ENTRANCED

THE SIOUXSIE & BANSHEES

STORY

Omnibus Press

LONDON — NEW YORK — SYDNEY — COLOGNE

Edited by Chris Charlesworth
Art Direction by Mike Bell
Book Designed by Liz Nicholson
Artwork by Tim Field
Picture Research by Debbie Dorman
Project and typesetting co-ordinated by Caroline Watson

ISBN 0.7119.1773.6 Order No: OP 45277

Exclusive distributors:
Book Sales Limited, 8/9 Frith Street, London W1V 5TZ, UK.
Music Sales Corporation, 225 Park Avenue South,
New York, NY 10003, USA.
Music Sales Pty Limited, 120 Rothschild Avenue,
Rosebery, NSW 2018, Australia.
To the Music Trade only:
Music Sales Limited, 8/9 Frith Street, London W1V 5TZ, UK.

Picture credits:
Every effort has been made to trace the
copyright holders of the photographs in
this book but one or two were unreachable.
We would be grateful if the photographers
concerned would contact us.

Typeset by Capital Setters, London
Printed in England by Courier
International Ltd. Tiptree, Essex.

Picture credits:
Peter Anderson: Inside Cover, p2, 5,
48, 50/51, 70, 76, 82, 83, 85, 86, 96
Adrian Boot: p28, 59
Erica Echenberg: p21
Fin Costello: p6, 22, 23, 24,
27, 35, 36, 42, 44, 45
The Face: p61
London Features Int:
p52, 54/55, 73, 75, 92, 93
NME: p63
Pictorial Press: p90/91
Barry Plummer: p10, 11, 17,
31, 33, 38(T&B), 39(T&B), 41, 78
Ray Stevenson: p9, 14, 18, 66

Contents

Foreword

"With skin as white as snow, hair as black as ebony, and lips as red as blood, she is the fairest of them all."

In the land of wicked witches, charming princes and poor serving wenches, these were assets that could lift a girl out of the gutter and into a magical world of sparkling diamonds, castles in the clouds and eternal enchantment. Or so it seemed.

Visit London's Camden Market and you could be forgiven for thinking that something very sinister happened to Snow White in the woods. In their twos and threes, they shuffle aimlessly from stall to stall, paying scant attention to anything that does not gleam like a studded belt, sparkle like a bevy of bracelets or resemble a can of hairspray. One or two might hover around the bootleg tape stalls which line the ever-bustling pavements of the High Street.

Dressed in regulation leather, lace or PVC or a combination of all three, black of course, they congregate like mourners at the funeral of Dr Phibes. Cut-price jewellery lends a glow of iridescence, fishnets a hint of fleeting sensuality. It is a peep show for some, maybe, but the overall air of impassive defiance is enough to unnerve Mr Jones into saving his customary wolf-whistles for more vulnerable looking victims.

The black hair, white faces and blood-red lips are still there, but these Snow Whites are a little less demure and no longer believe in happy endings. The image echoes a world of make-believe: mystery, from the East with kohl black eyes; magic, from precious stones and diamanté; signs and symbols that would make Aleister Crowley turn in his diabolic grave. Waiting for that handsome prince? I think not.

For surely it would take a new breed of handsome prince to look twice at these startling visions. And we've yet to mention their plumage. To call it a shock of hair would be clichéd if it wasn't such an exact description. Once only cartoon characters sported such gravity-defying barnets, and then, only after contact with some powerful electrical appliance. But today's ubiquitous crimping tongs have helped thousands of young women become photofit reconstructions of one of the most distinctive female personalities of our generation and, perhaps, beyond.

Visually Siouxsie Sioux may well be the Cleopatra of the technological age – always striking, often aped but never emulated – and it's possible that history will choose to remember this, rather than her avowed raison d'être, which is as lead singer with The Banshees, natch Siouxsie And The Banshees. Though other members have played their part in the band's success, there is little doubt that it is the power of her persona and the subconscious allure of her projection that is the central key to the continuing popularity of the group.

Having first entered the public eye as attention-seeking acolytes of that "nightmare of British culture", The Sex Pistols, the incipient Banshees soon forged a strong identity of their own. This enabled them to transcend the punk ghetto which had formed into line before you could say 'bandwagon'. Devoid of any character to call their own, the vast majority of these wannabees secured one-off deals, and were quickly discarded once the euphoria among A&R men wore off.

Meanwhile, Siouxsie And The Banshees were busy constructing their own fort from which to fight. And a battle it was. They had a unique sound, expressed total disdain for rock 'n' roll and its trappings, and were determined not to sell themselves short to record companies who saw punk rock as a quick way to a fast buck. But critics have made life hard for those from the Class Of '76 who dared to outstay their allotted 15 minutes. Many agreed with Julie Burchill when she discarded the likes of Jagger and Dylan with the clarion call to "Take these gods and stuff them!" But the idealism of the time has meant that punk – and its so-called 'survivors' – has had to bear a double-edged brunt. On the one hand, there were the revengeful purists who should have known better than to follow leaders, and the post-hippie drivel merchants (they never caught on until it was too late anyway) who smirked as the shock of the new began to blend comfortably with the complacency of the old.

While it would be unfair to single out Siouxsie And The Banshees as any more or any less competitive than the next group, no reading of their career could ignore the single-minded drive that has ensured their progress. From buying 'the best' records during their teens to following 'the best' band in 1976 they formed their own band which they believed, along with countless others, to be quite simply 'the best'.

The approachin

isease

When people visit Chislehurst, it's usually to see the caves. **When** Otherwise it's a typically dozy suburb, tucked away some 12 miles from the heart of London in the no-man's land just inside the Kent **We Were** borders; not exactly Stepford Wives, but relatively tranquil nevertheless. Unlike its counterparts in the north and western environs of the capital, the south-east is poorly served by the Underground **Young** tube system. So for many of the town's younger sons and daughters, city life retains a sense of mystery.

But Chislehurst does boast some fine parks and a wood; natural terrains where Janet Susan Ballion (the oft-quoted Dallion appears to be incorrect) spent much of her childhood, hoping to chance upon fairies, frogs and butterflies. Now, as Siouxsie Sioux, pop icon and undisputed beauty queen of the counter-culture, she is probably the town's most famous resident. Not that there's much competition. Spike Milligan spent a few weeks working in a laundry here many years ago but he soon moved on. Any ties with rock music are pretty slim too. Jimi Hendrix performed in the caves back in his early days and Led Zeppelin threw a party there to launch their Swansong label in 1974. A rock genealogist would do better to visit nearby Beckenham (David Bowie) or Dartford (Jagger and Richard). That is, until more recently.

In many ways the Ballions give the appearance of being just another English middle class family. Yet the unusual collection of ebony tribal masks adorning the wall space normally reserved for a Constable print suggest that the household was blessed with more than its fair share of cosmopolitanism. These were relics from a stay in the Belgian Congo where, rumour has it, Mr Ballion was – wait for it – a snake doctor. As the surname intimates, the family are of Belgian origin, and lived there for a while before moving to the Congo where Sioux's elder brother and sister were born.

But it is the less illustrious locale of Guy's Hospital, London, within earshot of Bow Bells, that marks the birthplace of the Ballions' youngest child. Born on May 27, 1957, Janet was just old enough to catch the wind of change that altered the life of a million teenagers during the sixties, but too young to be any part of it.

Broadstairs, the South-East seaside resort which provides East London families with a low-key holiday alternative to Margate and Ramsgate, has early pop connections for Sioux. It was here she saw her first concert – Cliff Richard at the Pavilion! – and on another occasion, she was coaxed on to a stage at a talent contest, but not even Adam Faith could persuade her to sing 'Baa Baa Black Sheep'. The tot remained silently stagestruck.

Pop music formed a backdrop to the lives of most children spawned in the late fifties: when she wasn't doting on her cats, throwing the javelin in school competitions or feigning suicide, the pre-pubescent Sioux would catch glimpses of *Ready Steady Go!*, television's premier pop showcase. Several years ago, she recalled The Troggs' vocalist Reg Presley coming on "completely over-the-top sexy!" during one programme. Apart from indicating an early awareness of carnal chemistry, it goes a long way to explaining her later fascination for Jim Morrison, lead singer of The Doors, who was rock's tragic Adonis.

Many traits and obsessions which today form a large part of the 'Sioux' persona have been clearly evident since childhood. It wasn't poverty or neglect that made her a latch-key kid, but an early desire to assert her independence. If she sulked on her first day at infants' school, it had little to do with missing mother. The plain fact was she didn't want to sit next to anyone. And yet in rejecting the sense of community offered by her family and school, the pre-pubescent rebel developed a special bond with her cats, Crystal and Cookie. "I like their temperament because they don't give a shit about anyone," she said.

The overall impression of the young Janet Ballion is that of a lonely child; and for one not long into the world, she quickly developed a fascination for ways of getting out of it: "At the age of six or seven, or it might have been younger, I tried to commit suicide with my mum's asthma pills. I wanted to get attention, I suppose. I used to drop books upstairs so they'd think I'd fallen down, then lie on the bed with a bottle of pills in my hand. But once I actually took them. I don't know whether I was thinking seriously about what I was doing . . . I thought I would succeed."

Already, her sense of the morbid was laced with more than a dash of the theatrical. And it wasn't long before she found certain kindred spirits – befriending a group of local gypsies and developing a rapport with some of her elder sister's friends (later she discovered most of her favourites were homosexuals). Since her sixth birthday brought with it an Indian squaw's outfit and a wigwam, she developed a passion for dressing up. This was no Milky Bar Kid. Her next birthday yielded the litter of kittens which were to become soulmates, and she has left traces of this admiration for the domestic cat on records, in photographs and on film. Mysterious, beautiful and independent, these creatures provide as good a role model for the future singer as any human could.

The usual teenage traumas did little to alter her basic instincts; in fact they strengthened them. Her response to the very major problem of what to do after leaving school was the classic one – boredom: "Before I was in a band, I only knew what I didn't want to do – everything that was offered to me!" If she fantasised about working in a zoo, becoming a surgeon, barmaid or hooker, it was probably a reaction to the more humble expectations held by her mother. As it turned out, she spent several months learning secretarial skills at Orpington College, before realising it was totally inappropriate to her needs.

During the mid-teen years the sex roles tighten. Many bow under the weight of peer group pressure; dissidents either opt out completely and hibernate, or else play the game on their own terms. Siouxsie quite clearly fell into the latter group, adopting a confrontational, if at the same time glamorous style: "I used to go out of my way to have very attractive hairstyles, very short, geometrically very ugly, cropped and very frightening to the opposite sex."

But perhaps the most traumatic experience came at the age of 14 with the death of her father. She once said her immediate reaction was to laugh, and that the event left her completely unmoved, but three years later, in 1981, time had tempered her reaction: "I was affected by my father's death. It doesn't hit you at first, but later in life it can lead to an obsession for a while. The Deceased One. He died in an armchair he always used in the living room. I went through a phase of sitting in it, after it happened, hoping something would occur – just sitting in the dark."

Shock manifests itself in many ways. Sioux responded by seeking out new adventures, making regular visits to the pubs and clubs of London, and becoming a familiar face in the city's bohemian and gay circles. After the abortive secretarial course, she left home at 17 to live closer to her new stamping ground. For a while she worked in a pub, but the loneliness of the clientèle quickly dampened her enthusiasm and the dole soon beckoned.

'Two-Tone' Steve in '76

Then there was a brief stint as a masseuse: kitsch value it had plenty of, but the reality proved far too humiliating and she was off by lunchtime. At about this time, a new rock group known as The Sex Pistols began to appear on the London club and college circuit. Sioux and her network of friends quickly latched on to them as the saving grace of their unfocused rebellion. Which they probably were.

Among this circle of friends was Steven Bailey, who first crossed Sioux's path during a Roxy Music concert at Wembley Arena, back in 1974. He was slightly older and though born and raised in Highgate, his teenage years were spent in Bromley, a short bus ride from Chislehurst. Though this move south was, according to Steve, "something to do with giving me a better education," it seems he spent much of his time sitting at David Bowie's old school desk waiting for inspiration. The *Little Red Schoolbook*, a radical text aimed at fanning the anti-establishment mood of the late sixties among the next generation, offered further distraction from his studies.

Consequently, his work began to suffer, but school became a lot more fun. Steve left in summer 1972, ''then spent the next three years drifting from one mundane job to another, until I decided not to work for anyone any more.''

During the mid-seventies, the teenage market was beginning to swell the dole queues and, political point-scoring aside, this was as much to do with increased expectations as it was with Britain's industrial slide. More and more felt less inclined to waste a lifetime away performing menial tasks for the sake of a redundant lifestyle which offered a car, 2.4 kids and *The Generation Game* at weekends. Rock music, more than anything else, provided an escape from all this and was the catalyst which cemented Sioux and Steve's friendship.

''I left school in the summer of 'Ziggy Stardust', 'Tago Mago' and 'Virginia Plain'.'' (Steve)

By 1972, Steve was a confirmed rockaholic. It was The Velvet Underground's 'White Light, White Heat' that did it, a year or so earlier. Now

Antecedents

widely recognised as a major influence, The Velvets had few supporters during the early seventies, or even back in the mid-sixties when they were a going concern. In fact there was very little going for them at all. They were on the wrong side of America for a start. The pop nerve centre had by-passed New York, choosing instead to leapfrog from Merseyside to San Francisco, pausing briefly in Detroit.

The period 1971-1973, now immortalised as 'the Glam Years', saw some strange bedfellows vying for chart success. In the vanguard were ex-underground figures like David Bowie and Marc Bolan who both shot to the top with a combination of good looks and a new-found rock 'n' roll sensibility. Clinging to their shirt-tails was a motley collection: relics from pre-Beatlemania like Paul Raven (Gary Glitter) and Shane Fenton (Alvin Stardust); art-school glam (Roxy Music), rock 'n' roll glam (Mott The Hoople) and teenybop glam (The Sweet).

Through the patronage of David Bowie, ex-Velvet Underground vocalist Lou Reed began to reach a new public. It was thanks to Bowie again that Iggy Pop, one-time leader of Detroit cult band The Stooges, re-emerged. The inquisitive among Bowie's following soon acquainted themselves with these mysterious, cultish precursors of Ziggy Stardust, and undoubtedly Sioux and Steve were among them.

All this can be set against the predominant musical currents in so-called respected circles. After bathing in a psychedelic haze for a few months in 1967, the future of pop mutated into a monster. In the US, country rock and the singer-songwriter vogue displaced wild acid jams, while in Britain 'progressive rock' reared its ugly head. If pop music had grown up, its middle-age spread was not a pretty sight.

Captain Beefheart

Both Steve and Sioux scoured programmes like *Top Of The Pops* and *The Old Grey Whistle Test* for a glimpse of their idols, but Steve, in addition to The Velvets and Stooges, had discovered a couple of lesser-known acts working further away from the rock mainstream. Captain Beefheart, unsurpassed to this day in showing what can be achieved with a basic guitar/bass/drums/vocal line-up, has had little obvious influence on the Banshee sound; but the effect of German outfit Can (an assortment of highly trained musicians, including a couple of Stockhausen students and a prize-winning conductor) is more immediately discernible. Steve's economical, rhythmic bass style owes a considerable debt to Holger Czukay ("Everything else is nonsense," he has said) and Can's use of polyrhythms and non-Western musical sources should be familiar to all Banshee fans.

While Steven Bailey digested the best of a flagging rock scene in his bedroom, Sioux's ambitions led her to a singing instructor, where she took a few lessons. After a lot of practice, and several amateur tapes, she felt confident enough to respond to some small-ads in the back of *Melody Maker*. Some of these threw up record producers too lazy to go out and hunt for talent; others were little more than schoolboy hard rock outfits. The spectacle of Sioux running through songs like Deep Purple's 'Smoke On The Water', then awaiting the verdict while the budding cock-rockers deliberated on the novelty value of a 'chick' singer, borders on the grotesque.

Unsurprisingly, the experience cooled her enthusiasm for a singing career. In those pre-Patti Smith years, a life in rock 'n' roll stank as far as women were concerned: "I was holding back because I was put off by every other girl that was trying to get into the music business. They were all manipulated by men, singing pretty songs. So I just waited for something to happen. And it did. Just at the right time."

"Ninety-nine per cent of punks conform to anything that's going." (Sioux, late '77)

There's A New Sensation

Before punk there was Bad Company. Ostensibly a 'super-group', this hard rockin', hard-livin' combo provided a shining example of how tedium had invaded the medium. Could Elvis, The Beatles, The Stones or even Jimi Hendrix really be blamed for this? And what of the golden boys of a year or two ago? Bowie had sold his soul to disco. After a clash of egos between the two Bryans, Ferry and Eno, the former emerged victorious and turned Roxy Music into a bland moneyspinner to finance his new career as a lounge lizard. Bolan binged on whatever he could lay his hands on. The rot had even spread to the periphery where both Beefheart and Can had signed to Virgin Records, never to repeat their former musical glories.

It was Mick Jagger who once said that rock was a dead end job for dead end people and, by 1976, it certainly looked that way. During the year, a group of executioners called The Sex Pistols were dispatched with orders to kill it off for good; or at least to chop away the dead wood. To this day, Rotten and Sioux, punk rock's leading male and female protagonists, despise the notion that they front 'rock' bands. Rising to fame on the back of a total disdain for rock 'n' roll clearly left its mark.

Though Ravensbourne College of Art, Chislehurst, was right on Sioux's doorstep, she missed the sixth public performance of The Sex Pistols, when they played there on November 6, 1975. Luckily Simon Barker, who had originally introduced Sioux and Steve at the Roxy Music gig, was there to witness the mass exodus while the band played. Before long, word got round about this quartet of upstarts who charged through a set based around sixties standards (The Stooges' 'No Fun', Who and Dave Berry hits). Such a brashness and lack of reverence sent most gig-goers to the bar or into a corner for a few soporific tokes.

Sex Pistols Matlock, Rotten, Cook and Jones

In February, Steve caught The Pistols supporting The Hot Rods at London's Marquee Club, a performance which got them banned from further appearances there. But what he witnessed were flying chairs, a topless dancer named Jordan (resembling a collision between Dusty Springfield and Warhol's movie camera) and a band with guts and personality. He was impressed enough to ring his best mate, Bill Broad, who soon realised that musical events in London were of far greater importance than completing his English Literature degree at Sussex University.

Soon, the coterie of friends from the south-eastern suburbs began to turn up at every Pistols gig, even venturing beyond the capital when the band secured bookings further afield. Before long, rock journalist Caroline Coon dubbed them the 'Bromley Contingent'. In the small, cliquey world of the incipient punk scene, this gave Sioux and Steve a certain notoriety, though they later grew to despise the label: "There was no such thing as the 'Bromley Contingent'," said Steve. "It was just a bunch of people drawn together by the way they felt and the way they looked. The Sex Pistols and gay discos were focal points."

Snappy media labels aside, they were a clearly identifiable bunch. They aped Rotten's example in assuming alter egos: Sue (Lucas) Catwoman, Billy (Broad) Idol, Debbie (Wilson) Juvenile, Berlin, Steve (Bailey) Havoc/ Spunka/Severin and (Janet Ballion) Suzi/Siouxsie. They also became living mannequins for Malcolm McLaren's Kings Road clothes shop Sex, which touted wares that were not always within the bounds of legality (in the summer of 1975, the shop was prosecuted for displaying an obscene T-shirt under the 1824 Vagrancy Act).

If the music of The Pistols gathered momentum as an antidote to the complacency of the rock aristocracy, then Sex reactivated an age-old adage, glamour as a revolt against everyday life, and moulded it to fit The Pistols' subversive image. They stocked a good selection of rubberwear and assorted 'mail-order only' fetish clothing, and marketed their own designs such as the infamous bondage trousers and T-shirts adorned with provocative sexual imagery. Sioux and Steve appeared in the tabloids sporting McLaren/Westwood garb, but because punk was taken by many to be a contempt for consumerism (the greatest fetish of them all), the Bromley crowd were as ignored as they were imitated.

In their autopsy of punk, *The Boy Looked At Johnny*, Julie Burchill and Tony Parsons (the Louella and Hedda of the pop world) took a sideswipe at Sioux and Steve by referring to the 'Contingent' as "a posse of unrepentant poseurs committed to attaining fame despite their paucity of any talent other than being noticed." And in a way they were right. Sioux had not persevered with her singing, Steve had barely touched an instrument, yet the pair still managed to blag a support slot at the forthcoming 100 Club Punk Rock Festival in September 1976.

Exposure

"It was meant to be our 15 minutes of fame, but we managed to sustain it for 10 years, which only goes to show how addictive dressing up and making a noise for a living can be."
(Sioux, 1986)

Sioux's love affair with the camera really began at The Sex Pistols' appearance at the Screen On The Green all-nighter, on August 29, 1976. Arriving at the cinema wearing a black plastic cupless bra, non-matching stockings and suspender belt, a polka-dot transparent **100 Club** plastic mac, stilettos and a swastika armband, her notoriety was assured among the rest of the audience who watched transfixed as she led the dance of the vampires to the sounds of Roxy Music and other acceptable golden oldies in between the live music. Thanks to the music press, always quick on the draw for an opportunity to publish a picture of a pair of breasts, Sioux's attire elevated The Pistols' mystique and gave her a first taste of media stardom.

Steve, by this time her constant companion, sat beside her. His newly-bleached hair spawned a temporary name-change, though in actual fact, Two-Tone Steve looked a dead ringer for Grandad from *The Munsters*.

A chat with Malcolm McLaren that night gave the couple their first stage break. Whether The Pistols' card holder offered them the chance to play voluntarily, or needed gentle arm-twisting, depends on who you choose to believe; either way, he knew that putting two of The Sex Pistols' earliest and most notorious followers on stage would further the cause which, by now, was poised to explode in the unsuspecting face of the British public.

Sioux and Steve were obviously delighted, even though the weekly arrival of a new batch of bandwagon hoppers since the summer had removed much of the exclusivity from what they felt was their movement. The pair have never hidden their contempt for many of these fellow travellers: "Punk died when The Damned played their first gig," one of them said.

Why The Banshees took so long to emerge has never been clear. Perhaps they thought punk would burn itself out; in any case, while new names like The Clash and The Buzzcocks quickly transformed enthusiasm into action, Sioux and Steve were content to bathe in their reputations as Pistols' devotees of the first order. And what better way to confirm this than by

On stage at The Screen On The Green, August '76

travelling abroad to witness the Foul-Mouthed Four's first overseas concerts. Together with a couple of others, Sioux and Steve crammed into the back of Billy Idol's ex-Post Office Morris van and made it in time for the two weekend shows at the Club de Chalet du Lac in Paris. Steve kitted himself out in a fetching purple and yellow toreador's outfit; Sioux stuck to the gear she had worn with such great effect at the Screen less than a week ago. But on this occasion someone took offence and lashed out at her. It wasn't the last time sartorial matters would lead to consternation.

On their return to England, the pair turned their attentions towards the impending date at the 100 Club. One night at Louise's, the Soho night club frequented by the Sex shop élite, Steve hit on a name. The Banshees. Suzi And The Banshees.

The pair knew that the punk rock 'movement' was already under threat: not from the righteous indignation of the national press, but from the Would-Be Rottens who observed the prototype, then sought to ape it. By taking to the stage with the sole intention of playing one number until the crowd threw them off, Suzi And The Banshees sought to prove a point to themselves, and to the phalanx of punk purists: "The point of that performance was simply that all the other bands were talking about not being able to really play, and being unrehearsed and into chaos, man, and we were simply doing what they were stating. Only they were really talking shit because they did rehearse and had worked up sets. We just wanted to take the whole thing to its logical extreme." (Sioux)

Things might have been very different had their old pal and would-be guitarist Billy Idol not let them down a week beforehand. The original idea was to play three of their most hated songs, the Bay City Rollers' 'Money Honey', the theme from the James Bond movie *Goldfinger* and the grossly over utilised 'Louie Louie'. Billy, a guitarist of some three or four years standing, would teach Steve just enough on bass not to look too stupid and the short set would be forgotten once they'd left the stage. But fearing for his image, and the reputation of his new band Chelsea, Bromley's blond bombshell pulled out and instead recommended Chelsea cast-off Marco Pirroni.

As the day of the gig drew closer, any hope of cobbling together a set faded quickly. Sioux was waitressing at the fashionable Valbonne club in the West End, and there was little time available to discuss what to play, let alone rehearse it. But they found a drummer in fellow Pistols acolyte, Sid Vicious, anxious to build himself a reputation equal to that of his Rotten sparring partner. Twenty-four hours before they were due to go on, these makeshift Banshees finally got it together at The Clash's rehearsal room in Camden. Attempting to work on songs at this late stage was obviously impractical, but setting 'The Lord's Prayer' to a barrage of improvised sound was not. Throw in a few lines from songs like 'Twist And Shout', 'Knocking On

Heaven's Door' and 'Goldfinger' and the twin birds of rock and religion could be struck with one sacrilegious stone.

The 100 Club's 'Punk Rock Festival', held over two nights in July, was a pivotal point in the history of the burgeoning movement. On the scent of a quick buck, the A&R men who descended on Oxford Street stuck out a mile amid the weird assortment of enthusiasts who had latched onto the new cult. Within a couple of weeks The Sex Pistols had secured a handsome £40,000 advance from EMI and the gates were flung open. Sid Vicious did his reputation no harm by 'inventing' the pogo dance during the course of events, though allegations that it was his glass-smashing enthusiasm during The Damned's set on the second night can't have impressed the girl whose eye was pierced by a stray fragment. Punk became front page news and was banned from the club.

The Banshees' set was no less eventful. Even before they walked on stage, Clash manager Bernie Rhodes took offence at Sioux's swastika armband and refused to allow his band's distinctive luminous pink equipment to be associated with the symbol. The Pistols had no such qualms and averted disappointment by lending their gear. When The Banshees finally appeared, Marco, Steve and Sid looked the part with their de rigueur Union Jack and Karl Marx pin-ons and paint-splashed shirts. Sioux, meanwhile, left her under-dressed look in her wardrobe and opted for an Oxfam-style man's suit. The armband remained as a token gesture to outrage.

At London's 100 Club, Sid, Steve and Sioux

They carried out their planned improvisation based around 'The Lord's Prayer', though the performance didn't go quite to plan: ''The intention was to play one number until they threw us off the stage,'' said Sioux, ''but they never did . . . We got bored before them.'' It was more likely a mistaken gesture from Marco to Steve that prematurely ended the set. Whatever the case, people began to talk about Suzi And The Banshees. ''When we came off I knew,'' remarked the non-bass-playing bassist. And Sioux could see her cheerleader days fading into the distance: ''For the first time ever, I felt part of what was going on,'' she said.

Audience reaction to the onslaught was unsurprisingly polarised. They had the blessing of the movement's undisputed figurehead, Johnny Rotten, who allegedly danced his way to the front of the stage, but to the massed ranks of talent scouts present they were box office poison. ''God it was awful,'' said Island's Howard Thompson. And that swastika! As someone once observed, not even record companies could sell fascism. Though it was the first and only time Sioux wore it on stage, it was to prove the band's bugbear for well over a year.

Original Banshees fan Nils Stevenson

Nils Stevenson, a McLaren sidekick who like Sioux and Steve was an Old Pistolian, became The Banshees' biggest champion. Today he's reticent, almost embarrassed by the whole affair, but back then his enthusiasm for the 100 Club performance knew no bounds: ''What a gig!'' he wrote in the text for his brother Ray's photo-history of the group. ''I just went mad about them. It was the greatest thing I'd seen since Iggy played at the King's Cross cinema in '72.'' Nils obviously fancied himself as a Svengali and Malcolm had advised him to take on Subway Sect. But there was no contest: his belief in the potential of The Banshees, and particularly the singer, was enormous. She couldn't sing, the band couldn't play; but this budding Mickie Most of the new wave recognised Star Quality when he saw it. His passion for the group almost got the better of him when he fancied himself as the band's guitarist, but he soon settled down to the role of manager.

The first problem facing Sioux, Steve and Nils was simple: find a new drummer and guitarist. The informal nature of The Banshees' début performance meant there were no obligations. Sid broke away to form the Flowers Of Romance, though he settled several months later for a co-starring role as bassist with The Sex Pistols. On the other hand, Marco didn't quite fit in with the image The Banshees attempted to portray, and he was gently nudged into pursuing a managerial role with The Slits. This didn't come off but Marco found belated success three years later as the musical brain behind Adam And The Ants.

There were no more sonic assaults from Suzi And The Banshees for six months, though the unholy trinity were far from idle. Neither were they out of the news. Sioux and Steve were among the fans present during The

Sex Pistols' notorious appearance on *The London Weekend Show* hosted by Bill Grundy. Towards the end of the show, Grundy turned his attentions to Sioux, and it was his antiquated innuendos that provided the cue for the short burst of profanities which transformed The Pistols into nationwide heroes/public enemy number one overnight.

Punk held the front pages for days, and on December 3, the *Daily Mirror* printed a large picture of a grimacing female alongside the headline 'Siouxsie's A Punk Shocker'. She told them that The Sex Pistols were "the first group that has got around to saying or doing anything worthwhile," and that she'd drunk too much "fire water" before the Grundy show. Her front page appearance resulted with her dismissal from the Valbonne and, presuming a 'singer' to be earning a good wage, the DHSS put a stop to her dole money.

A support slot on The Sex Pistols' Anarchy In The UK Tour, which was scheduled to run from December 3-26, was allegedly declined by the remaining Banshees. Nils went along in his capacity as road manager but left a key with Sioux and Steve. This gave them unlimited entry to the small room above 6 Denmark Street which, as well as providing shared living accommodation for Nils and Pistols' guitarist Steve Jones, doubled up as The Sex Pistols' rehearsal room. The Banshees called up an old friend, Peter (P.T.) Fenton, who played guitar but possessed only a bass; though punk activist Mark P., who had just started *Sniffin' Glue* fanzine, helped by donating a guitar. Sometime during the run-up to Christmas, both Sioux and Steve underwent a name change. Hers was a simple spelling alteration though it did affect the group name. His choice of surname dated back to his passion for The Velvet Underground, who on 'Venus In Furs' (based on the Sacher-Masoch novel of the same title) sang of a character named 'Severin'.

Although Nils wanted Sid to stay on, ("He was a much better drummer than bass player," said Sioux), another 100 Club convert, Kenny Morris, talked his way on to the vacant stool. Actually, a chap called Dixon (a throwback to the liner notes of the first Roxy Music album if ever there was one) auditioned first but he couldn't play. Kenny was no Ginger Baker either, but there were two things in his favour: he didn't like using cymbals, and with his short, dark hair and finely chiselled features, he bore an uncanny resemblance to Sioux.

The Banshees now consisted of a drummer whose chief influences were The Velvets' Maureen Tucker and The Glitter Band, a bassist who could barely venture further than the top string and a singer who saw no reason to waver from the one-dimensional wail she'd hit upon. They could either play safe, or hope their untrained minimalism would lead to a style of their own. For the time being, the former sufficed.

No doubt they were hoping for a touch of the John Cale's when violinist Simone joined these preliminary musical adventures. But she stayed for only two rehearsals. It was another five years before Siouxsie And The Banshees would again call upon a violin. For the moment, they swam with the tide; a demo tape recorded for Track Records in June bears this out.

Money was extremely tight. Nils had been sacked by McLaren for allowing his protégés into The Pistols' Tin Pan Alley hideaway, though he did have £600 savings (boosted by a £300 pay-off from his old boss) which could be called upon in an emergency. But luckily he found himself a job entirely compatible with his ambitions for the band. Well-known rock 'n' roll degenerate Johnny Thunders, together with his Heartbreakers, had signed to Track Records having returned from the abortive Anarchy Tour and Stevenson managed to get himself taken on as an A&R consultant for the label. In addition to £20 a week, use of a company phone and a roof over his head (sharing a Pimlico flat with the hard living New Yorkers), he persuaded Track to finance some of The Banshees' bills while he looked elsewhere for a deal. It was a poorly-kept secret that the label formed by former Who managers Chris Stamp and Kit Lambert in 1967 was running on borrowed time.

The new-look Banshees premièred at the Red Deer pub in suburban Croydon, not far from the stamping ground of their early teens. It was the first of two engagements supporting The Heartbreakers, though they blew out the Americans' Chinese Rocks Tour in the spring. The next couple of gigs found them supporting The Slits, an all-girl punk outfit whose performances were chaotic affairs. Basic as it was, The Banshees did at least have a set.

A rare shot with P.T. Fenton on guitar in early 1977

Sign The
Banshees

The six songs that made up the band's original set that spring were recorded as a demo for Track Records at the Riverside Studios on June 12 (not March as is widely thought). After the label went into liquidation later that year, the masters disappeared; however, rough copies of the proceedings have been grist to the bootlegger's mill, and have since been widely circulated.

Guitar and vocals dominate the primitive recording, though the preoccupations betrayed by songs like 'Captain Scarlett', 'Bad Shape' and '20th Century Boy' still remain a vital part of the Banshee credo; namely childhood, misanthropy and the rock of their teenage years. The guitar and voice worked unspectacularly in tandem, as evidenced on a song such as 'Psychic', which was barely more than a prototype for groups like Sham 69 to follow. But the negativity was instantly refreshing: 'We're all fucking spastics, we're all mongoloids,' screamed Sioux on 'Bad Shape', and few disputed her sincerity.

'Grammar Boy' Steve

A performance at the Roxy Club, the Covent Garden mecca for aspiring punk acts, was filmed by Don Letts, though omitted from his rarely-screened fly-on-the-wall documentary, *The Punk Rock Movie* in favour of clips filmed during The Heartbreakers' tour later that year. There is little evidence of the cold, calculated aura projected by, or for, the group by the year's end; instead we see an enthusiastic run through 'Bad Shape' and 'Limblessly In Love' (later retitled 'Carcass') and some backstage sideswipes at Roxy Club owner, Andy Czezowski.

EMI recorded several bands at the Roxy during March and April, including The Banshees, and wanted to include at least one of their songs on a forthcoming compilation, 'Live At The Roxy, London WC1'. The band were not keen on the idea and the tapes stayed in the can. At the end of 1988, these recordings were exhumed and touted for possible release. If so, we would hear the same six-song live set performed throughout the spring of 1977. Rough, distinctive but not yet unique, it would at last give Pete Fenton some hard vinyl proof that he was once a Banshee.

Since shunning the Sex shop style which by now the flock had adopted, Steve looked more like a grammar school boy fresh out of uniform than the punk shocker splashed across the tabloids, decked out in full regalia two-tone hair, handcuffs, safety pins, curtain runners, paper clips, paint, the lot. But Fenton was the man out of place; he was the band's Glen Matlock. His guitar-playing was functional he rattled out the chords as well as the next amateur but was far too 'rock 'n' roll'; the aspirations of Sioux, Severin and Morris stretched way beyond that.

Yet it could so easily have been Kenny Morris. Nils had spent hours persuading record company scouts that Dingwalls on May 19 was a must for their diary. Forget the 100 Club, he told them. (If only he knew he'd be saying the same thing a year later!) This band is it! But Kenny wasn't coming. He was miles away, in Battersea, bed-ridden and sweating out a fever. Nils and Sioux drove down and convinced him that, fever or no fever, he was playing that evening. As it turned out, Kenny's only mishap was falling off his stool; it was Peter's performance which had Nils hiding under tables by the end of the evening. He lasted just long enough to record the demo for Track and was out by the start of July.

If it hadn't been for Dave Woods (the band's agent since March) opening his own Vortex club, Siouxsie And The Banshees would have been hard pressed to find work, having practically rendered themselves unbookable after the Dingwalls debacle. But it wasn't just their competence that was being questioned.

"Outrage is the game, Siouxsie And The Banshees is the name," ran the lead-in to Jane Suck's article in *Sounds* towards the end of June. The feature went on to depict the group as a bunch of Jew-hating intolerants with a penchant for cheapo horror stories and laughing at spastics. A few weeks earlier, a reviewer in *NME* wrote: "If they ever have another Nuremburg Rally, Siouxsie And The Banshees will be there." The group's response to the Suck feature was printed in a future *Sounds* letters page: "We are not Nazis," they wrote, "and we are getting pissed off for being shunned because of misquotes by sensation-seeking reporters we don't need it!"

Of course the band weren't Nazis; but they did want to have their cake and eat it. They were, after all, not only the children of Johnny Rotten but of David Bowie too. Sioux and Steve may have taken to following The Pistols around by May 1976, but when their old idol announced a series of six nights at the Empire Pool, Wembley his first UK dates since the Ziggy retirement show in July 1973 they rushed for tickets.

As the year progressed, hardly a word was written about the Banshees without alluding to their allegedly Nietzschean nature. Nils was unhappy about the line in 'Love In A Void' and remembers it being the cause of many an argument: "It almost got to the point where it was, 'Stop all that or I'm leaving'," he said. By the year's end, the message finally got through, and *Sounds* Vivien Goldman was the first to know: "That (line's) gonna be changed when we think of something to put in, but it was never meant to be anti-Semitic," Steve told her, before Sioux piped in with a dubious analogy that, "Too many Jews means, like, too many fat businessmen."

But mud sticks and Siouxsie And The Banshees – with the exception of The Slits – were the last among the class of '76 to secure a record deal. Yet throughout 1977, they had developed a substantial following on the club circuit where they broke attendance records at the Vortex, financed their own provincial UK tour and made a brief sojourn across the channel for a few dates. Quite an achievement for a band without a drum-kit or amplifier to call their own. And they had established a musical direction. The Siouxsie And The Banshees of December 1977 was a far greater beast than the derivative creature of six months earlier. After all, they now had a songwriter within their ranks.

John McKay had travelled down from his native Hemel Hempstead many times to see the group, and when he heard Fenton was out, approached Kenny Morris with a view to an audition. His moody good looks, stylish manner and off-beat approach to the guitar endeared him to the others, and a week later the new-look outfit made a low-key appearance at the Shad Thames warehouse in Butler's Wharf, East London. The occasion was a party hosted by underground darlings Andrew Logan and film-maker Derek Jarman, the latter talent-spotting for his forthcoming punk-inspired movie *Jubilee*. Also on the bill were Wayne County, The Rich Kids and Gloria Mundi, though only the first-named ended up in the film.

John McKay

Kenny Morris

Jarman was keen to secure the involvement of The Banshees, but apart from Kenny (who, together with his friend John Maybury, helped build some of the sets), they refused. "We'd seen the script and some rushes," said Sioux, who continued: "Its only motivation was money, it was a total cash-in, totally decadent and totally unreal." Nevertheless Jarman used a snatch of 'Love In A Void' transmitted on a TV set during the movie. This wasn't filmed on the night of the party: on that occasion they played a 10-minute set consisting of a version of The Beatles' 'Helter Skelter' which segued into 'The Lord's Prayer'.

Not long after John's arrival, two other songs began to appear in their set. One was a black tale of a butcher's assistant, who fell in love with the carcasses he worked with and ended up chopping off his own limbs, then skewering himself on to the meat-hooks to be near them. Less macabre was 'Make Up To Break Up' which was merely a cautionary tale of a physiognomical nature.

The group performed 'Make Up' on the provincial TV pop programme *So It Goes*, but it was a session recorded for the influential late night Radio One host John Peel that gave them their first national exposure. Nils had approached Peel several times at the Vortex with a view to securing a session but he lacked the McLaren touch. It took some careful manoeuvring on the part of Dave Woods to finally crack it. The band did the rest – the session was a revelation.

Of the four songs taped, three – 'Metal Postcard', 'Suburban Relapse' and 'Mirage' – were McKay compositions, with lyrics by Sioux or Steve. Only a vastly improved 'Love In A Void' survived from the Fenton days. Peel had been broadcasting sessions by dozens of new wave bands throughout the year but nothing compared with this. Musically, 1977 ensured that the likes of Iggy, The New York Dolls and The Velvets were rewritten into rock's back pages, but few had managed to forge a particularly new style. Throbbing Gristle and This Heat made dissenting noises on the fringe but the freshness within the mainstream was sustained by Siouxsie And The Banshees.

BBC sessions are always recorded with a minimum of fuss and the economic production suited the band's uncluttered sound. Morris' drums were given The Glitter Band treatment on 'Love In A Void', while controversy was avoided by the substitution of the word 'quacks' instead of 'Jews'; 'Mirage' was an instantly memorable pop song of the first order, but it was the remaining songs which best defined the unmistakable Banshee sound. Drawing heavily on Bowie's futuristic scenarios, 'Metal Postcard' hung on an unrelenting clockwork rhythm, with Sioux providing the emotionless, clipped overtones. 'Suburban Relapse' was something else again. Starting out with some punishingly effective double-tracked guitar, the song invoked the nightmare that lurks just under the skin of day-to-day normality, and pushed it to the extreme with some agonising changes in pace. Behind every dream house a bleak house and didn't they know it! The group were no longer punk's unwanted ideologues but the spearhead of the so-called New Music. It had taken a year to get there. They now had a hard core of followers, won over thousands more with the Peel broadcast in December and found new champions among the music press; yet they were no closer to securing a record deal, which was the main objective. But it wasn't for want of publicity. An enthusiastic fan called Les Mills had seen to that. One October morning, employees of some 15 record companies arrived at their London offices to find a simple message sprayed on the wall of the entrance: Sign The Banshees. Do It Now. But for the time being, their cheque books remained closed. Les got his just rewards, though, joining the band as roadie/personal assistant before going on to manage The Psychedelic Furs.

If The Banshees' quest for a record deal became something of a cause célèbre, then there were reasons other than being 'untouchable' that denied them a home. A prevailing attitude among the major companies was that they only needed one 'punk' act. Many thought and hoped the new wave would quickly burn itself out and didn't wish to over-commit themselves. Of course, pride-swallowing, one-off deals of the kind offered by Decca to Adam And The Ants were common, but The Banshees weren't interested: "There's no reason why anyone shouldn't give us a human deal. We want to have control over everything that goes out under our name, every advert, every sleeve, because it's representing part of us. Why should we allow someone else to stick in a glossy picture of Sioux when it's got nothing to do with what we're doing?" (Steve)

The obvious answer would have been to team up with one of the rising independent companies, or better still, form their own label. Steve didn't see it that way: "It would be pointless to have that freedom and not be heard. I mean, the important thing is to get into a big record company and do the damage there."

But during the early months of 1978, the band seriously discussed going it alone. John Peel had been inundated with requests to repeat the session and his producer, John Walters, suggested they negotiate a deal with BBC Records to issue a song from their second session, broadcast in February, as a single. The track in question was 'Hong Kong Garden', an obviously commercial proposition with its oriental guitar hook. The three other cuts, 'Carcass', 'Overground' and 'Helter Skelter', only served to hasten The Banshees' ever-growing cult reputation.

Just as an arrangement with the BBC looked on the cards, several of the big companies began to make enquiries. John Darnley, an executive at EMI was keen to sign the band but had to back out when his peers got cold feet. RCA made enquiries but opted for Gloria Mundi instead. While The Banshees were getting near on 1000 people coming to their big gigs, Mundi were, in Nils' words, "drawing 20 at the Vortex." Atlantic A&R man Dave Dee rejected them because he felt punk was finished, Anchor decided they weren't rock 'n' roll enough and Chrysalis wouldn't even come to see them because they didn't like the name. It was a cruel world.

Then Decca stepped in with a disparaging offer which included an advance of £5,000 against an album. More serious negotiations began with Andrew Lauder's Radar label which had a distribution deal with WEA in the UK, but their lack of an outlet in the US proved to be a major stumbling block.

There had also been some preliminary discussions with Rough Trade, an independent company which was establishing a distribution network in order to avoid going cap in hand to one of the majors. Ever competitive, and acutely aware of their own importance, the band backed off. Self-esteem dictated that Siouxsie And The Banshees weren't going to be stigmatised as yet another punk band who failed to secure a 'proper' record deal.

Disappointed but undeterred, they embarked on a self-financed, 16-date tour at the end of March. Older material like 'Captain Scarlett', 'Psychic' and 'Scrapheap' had been jettisoned and the set now revolved around the eight tracks recorded for Peel, two new tracks, 'Pure' and 'Nicotine Stain', plus the inevitable 'The Lord's Prayer'.

The tour was received by enthusiastic audiences and kept the band in the news; though this was not particularly difficult as controversy continued to shadow Sioux's every move. During the past six months she had managed to get herself and Kenny arrested and later charged with obstruction of the highway. This incident occurred outside the Rainbow after her protestations at the heavy-handed treatment of 999's drummer by some over-zealous custodians of the law. Another mishap saw an unfortunate stage-hopper caught full in the face with the base of her mike stand in Amsterdam; and she overshadowed *The Great Rock 'n' Roll Swindle* movie première by getting thrown out of a Wardour Street pub for wearing one of McLaren/Westwood's less salubrious T-shirts. She's outrageous, she screams and she bawls. But who'd have a lass insane?

Nils Stevenson first cultivated the acquaintance of Alan Black, A&R at Polydor, after gatecrashing the label's staff Christmas party. But it took weeks of pestering before Black agreed to see him in an official capacity. Nils seized the opportunity, and turned up with an impressive folio of cuttings, photographs and a recent tape of the band. It did the trick. Black called in Chris Parry from an adjoining office and secured his blessing to negotiate a deal. Apparently, Radar were contacted in case they could come up with a better offer, but within a week the quartet walked through the doors at Stratford Place, and came out a few inches taller as contracted Polydor recording artistes.

Hallowed be thy

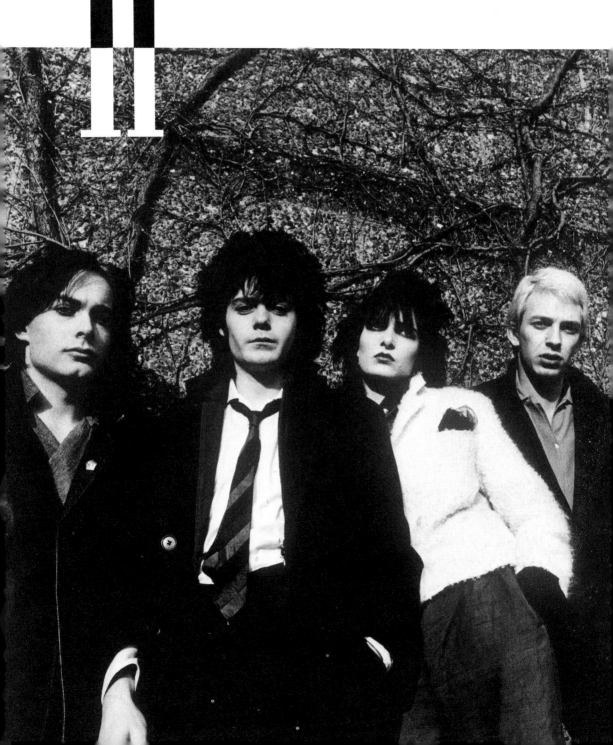

m e

"It would be nice to turn on the radio one day and hear ourselves." (Sioux)

After a year-and-a-half of false starts, blind alleys and endless gigging, The Banshees had overcome the major hurdle of their career: but this was no time for complacency. They had the deal they wanted; the next challenge was to seal it with a hit record. On June 17, little over a week after signing, work began on their first single 'Hong Kong Garden'.

The Scream Of The Iron Butterfly

Recording a song which they'd perfected live over a period of six months, and had already taped for the BBC, proved more difficult than envisaged. Polydor had flown in soul producer Bruce Albertine from the States but it was an inappropriate – and costly – choice. In Trident Studios, one of the most expensive in London, all that was achieved in two days was a half-decent drum sound. Albertine had no empathy with the group's approach at all: his natural habitat was dealing with top session musicians, certainly not with a drummer who couldn't tune his kit. After running up a bill of £12,000, they came out with an unbearable version of what should have been their flagship.

Polydor were quite prepared to release this travesty but the band were not. They moved quickly, courted Steve Lillywhite (who'd kept order during the recent Johnny Thunders sessions) in a pizza house, then sent him home with a pile of carefully selected records to digest. In a far less palatial atmosphere than that afforded to Albertine, Lillywhite engineered a sound better suited to the band's requirements – an upfront mix, plenty of top and bottom, and heavily echoed drums which gave a sense of space.

'Hong Kong Garden' was by no means the band's best song, but like their reputation and even their name, it was enigmatic and full of (Far Eastern) enchantment. The flipside, 'Voices', was salvaged from the abortive Albertine sessions, and was its antithesis. If the single was classy pop in the tradition of their early seventies' mentors, 'Voices' came as a savage assault on unsuspecting ears. Opening with a fanfare that echoed one of Can's wild rhythmic pulses, it soon mutated into an agonisingly slow number, where Sioux intoned at her ghostly best over a heavily flanged guitar refrain. The singer later recalled 'Voices' being a favourite with pub landlords who played the song in a last-ditched attempt to clear stragglers from the bar.

In many establishments, selecting it on the jukebox was a waste of five pence, because some smart alec would always nudge the machine to the cheers of the mob. Before long, the complaining public would succeed in getting the record removed.

'Hong Kong Garden' received its national première on Mickie Most's short-lived *Revolver* TV show in July, and on release in August, found its way on to the Radio One playlist and into the charts. Its success exceeded even the band's expectations: "We were surprised it got to number seven but we knew it was gonna be a hit," said the bassist. Sioux unashamedly recalls being "excited at the time," but McKay remained cynical and unmoved: "The Silver Disc was like one of those little gold stars – you get a pat on the head and a little gold star like at primary school. It was a bit ridiculous. They were going to present it, but we refused any presentation. It's a pretty bizarre thing to have. It doesn't mean anything to what we're doing, it's just part of the record company clockwork machinery. It keeps them happy."

After signing to Polydor the band concentrated all their efforts on recording, though once 'Hong Kong' was in the bag, they took a few days off to prepare for a major headlining appearance at the Roundhouse. After a warm-up gig at the Russell Club in Manchester, they opened the packed London engagement with a new composition called 'The Staircase (Mystery)', before running through finely tuned versions of their usual set. Two more songs were premièred that night, 'Jigsaw Feeling' and 'Switch'. Only two more appearances preceded the release of their début LP. On the day 'Hong Kong' was issued, they headlined the opening night of the Edinburgh Rock Festival; and a month later, played the Aylesbury Friars, a popular out-of-town venue for a low-key concert.

By the end of August, Siouxsie And The Banshees had completed the final stages of their album and were already lining up a major UK tour to coincide with its release. A touch of the Rod Stewart's? Siouxsie And The Banshees were never revolutionaries; if they arrived at Polydor in a Trojan Horse, it quickly became a red herring. They entered the heart of the beast for no greater purpose than to further their own musical ambitions. Punk's dichotomy was that it highlighted the various power relationships involved in the rock process, but none of the major protagonists possessed the will to challenge them, save for a few token clauses allowing them a say in the design of their record sleeves and such like. But even if Siouxsie And The Banshees had no lofty ideas about altering the symbiotic nature of the pop game, they were not about to become a mere footnote in the here-today, gone-tomorrow rock world.

'The Scream' ensured there would be no danger of that. It was undoubtedly one of the most important albums of the seventies, up there with The Clash's eponymous début, Patti Smith's 'Horses', Bowie's 'Diamond Dogs' and the first long player from Jonathan Richman And The Modern Lovers.

Its sound was hard, metallic, ultra modern, and a far cry from the rock 'n' roll punk bands like Sham 69 and the other sub-Pistol parodies. And unlike other malcontents at the time The Banshees' music was reaching a wide audience. Maybe not as wide as drummer Kenny would have liked, ("The best thing for this album would be if couples sat down by the fireside and listened to it. It's those sort of people who need to listen to it,") but they weren't just preaching to the converted. That was the idea behind getting the backing of Polydor, a major company who could place full-page adverts in the weekly music press, and finance major national tours and promotional jaunts abroad.

No doubt our humanist friends would regard 'The Scream' as a collection of morbid vistas riddled with misanthropy. If so, they are not necessarily wide of the mark. The themes of alienation, despair and uncertainty that appeared with such gusto have become a trademark of the band's ever since, and led directly to the 'gothic' tag. But if they shared similar cultural references with the likes of Poe, then they were no different to many of the creative giants of the twentieth century. Rock, once purely a sacred altar for celebration, could now fall into line. The group smirked and thought to themselves: "This ain't rock 'n' roll, this is genocide!"

"Who wants to be David Bowie when they grow up?" taunted Julie Burchill, at the start of a review in which she flung everything she could at the band. It was her only constructive comment, but even then, she completely missed the point: this was the album Bowie should have made after 'Diamond Dogs'.

It opened with 'Pure', an instrumental so brief that this had to be a concept album. Unfolding like a rose, it quickly crescendoed into a cacophonous wail of harsh guitars and screams, and begged the listener to grasp hold of the stem. The first prickle, 'Jigsaw Feeling', was the vital one; still the prototype Banshees song, it found the band at their primitive best. Crashing drums, sheets of ear-splitting white noise guitar, a moody, no-nonsense bass-line and histrionic vocals from Sioux like a wound-up Nico – aloof yet vibrant, and resolutely impassive. The jigsaw feeling would crop up again and again in the band's work – confusion, states of near madness, the unconscious decision to be out of control. It was a universal one in other art forms – painting, film, classical music. The Banshees ensured it a prominent foothold in rock; though later they would be forced to shoulder the blame for an onslaught of goth imitators following in their wake.

Attention turned from 'self' alienation to that of a more general kind with 'Overground', the pressures to 'live a life of pleasantries, mingle in the modern families.' No matter that Sioux's voice was no great shakes at this stage; its starkness enabled her to deliver the song without a trace of self-pity. Similarly, the black wit of 'Carcass' was delivered dead-pan. A final touch of noir was the reference to 'carcrash' on the lyric sleeve which stemmed from a discussion with a fan after a concert.

Side one ended with the only cover version on the album, 'Helter Skelter', which was now so much part of the band that it had taken over from 'The Lord's Prayer' as their quintessential offering. In many ways it has remained so.

The second side began with what has generally become known as the single that got away, 'Mirage'. Apparently, Polydor were keen on releasing a hasty follow-up to 'Hong Kong Garden' and 'Overground' was suggested. The Banshees weren't sold on the idea at all, but made it clear that their choice would be 'Mirage'. At the time, their aversion to issuing album tracks as singles meant that neither saw the light of day; if they had their time again, 'Mirage' would almost certainly be released. Musically, it was the lightest track on the album, though once again, the preoccupation was with estrangement. Sandwiched between the twin pillars of strength that were 'Metal Postcard' (dedicated to anti-Nazi propagandist John Heartfield) and 'Suburban Relapse' (listen closely and you'll hear the sounds of every hermit's nightmare – the doorbell and the 'phone), was another relative newcomer to The Banshees' repertoire, 'Nicotine Stain'. If there was a weak link on the album, this Sioux/Severin composition was it. On any other record, it would have sounded a cut above the norm, but it was belittled in the context of 'The Scream'.

'Switch', the band's unwitting stab at progressive rock (a movement in three parts!), was taken by many to point to new horizons. It was a kind of open-ended conclusion: a savage indictment of 'progress', the checkmate situation implicit in a nuclear society. As on the previous track, John McKay augmented the sound with some restrained sax; otherwise they stuck to the usual rock 'n' roll four-piece format, In all, 'The Scream' was a remarkable achievement for a group who could hardly play their instruments a year or so earlier. It left one major problem – topping it.

On The Road Again

The fallacy that the spirit of '77 had opened up people's tastes and interests to any great degree was savagely exposed at the very start of The Banshees' first British tour of major venues during October and November. Bored with the usual fare of support acts, they recruited a little-known Birmingham-based duo called Spizz Oil (whose peculiar brand of DIY rock involved a guitar, a kazoo and some tuneless, if occasionally amusing anthems) to open the shows. The audiences' initial bemusement at the customised outfits and construction workers' helmets, turned sour after a few verses of songs like '6000 Crazy', 'Fibre' and '1989'. If this was the sound of the future, they weren't having any, and throughout the tour, Spizz and his partner Pete Petrol bravely continued in the face of some vicious heckling.

The other support act booked was Nico, one-time chanteuse for The Velvet Underground, whose enigma outshone the rest of Warhol's superstars put together. Since her split from The Velvets in 1967, she had embarked on an occasional solo career, though much of her time was spent in the shadows working on obscure foreign movies or inhabiting the nether-world invoked by serious drink and drug abuse. Sioux, Steve, Kenny and John must have felt they'd really made it. Nico as a warm-up act for Siouxsie And The Banshees? After you, divine enfante!

Nico: This femme fatale proved too much for Banshee audiences

But this teaming was too good for mere mortals. After only a couple of appearances, spent trying to avoid a hail of bottles, cans, fag-ends and whatever else the mob could fling, the German angel of doom was taken off the tour for her own safety. At the Cardiff Top Rank, where she managed four or five songs, a rolled-up missile of chewing gum got caught in her hair and had to be cut away on stage. "If I had a machine gun, I would shoot you all," she told them, then made her exit. She still managed a smile: after all, The Velvets weren't exactly the most popular act in their day either.

Even after Manicured Noise and the then-unknown Human League had deputised for Nico, the rest of the tour wasn't entirely trouble-free. After a soundcheck at the Glasgow Apollo, they returned to their hired Mercedes limousine to find it wrecked. Not only were the tyres let down, it was also heavily dented, covered in rubbish and had the words 'Capitalist Bastards' etched into the paintwork. The group's immediate reaction was to burst out laughing despite waving goodbye to their £1,500 deposit. They weren't afraid of getting up people's noses. Part of the rationale for hiring the limo was to go against the grain of street credibility cultivated by the likes of The Clash, The Jam and Sham 69. Of course comfort and speed were two more practical reasons. A replacement van was located and swapped for a more civilised mode of transport as soon as possible.

During the tour they took time out to record two songs, 'Metal Postcard' and 'Jigsaw Feeling', to revive BBC 2's flagging *Old Grey Whistle Test* broadcast on November 11. But their minds were firmly concentrated on new material. After the massive effort normally required to break into the mainstream, the tendency once the goal is achieved, is to breathe a proverbial sigh of relief. Consequently, second albums are very often a disappointment. Anyone in doubt should consult The Clash's 'Give 'Em Enough Rope' for confirmation. But it didn't have to be that way: genuine talents like Wire improved enormously as they perfected their craft.

The Banshees' problem was that they'd had two years to perfect theirs. Now they were required to come up with something within a matter of months (despite the control over their output, there were of course, certain contractual obligations); on top of that they had the added distraction of being a full-time professional outfit locked on a roundabout of promotional commitments. They may have by now been branded 'The Most Elitist Band In The World', but acquiring the oxygen of publicity was as time-consuming as it was laborious.

This wasn't always so. A follow-up to 'Hong Kong Garden' was in the bag before Christmas, and after a seasonal interlude, The Banshees began the first few weeks of 1979 in Europe, where they visited Paris, Hamburg and Berlin. New songs like 'Playground Twist', 'Placebo Effect' and 'Mittageisen', a German-language version of 'Metal Postcard', were sharpened, alongside 'Premature Burial' and 'The Staircase (Mystery)', which had both appeared in the set for several months by this time.

On their return, they expected to see 'The Staircase (Mystery)' in the shops. Instead pressing plant problems delayed the release until March, when its arrival left many slightly disappointed. Though the track had a gestation period of some six months, it never quite gelled, despite the recruitment of Marc Bolan's engineer Mike Stavrou to beef up the sound. (Much was made of the Bolan connection, especially with the band's pedestrian cover of '20th Century Boy' on the flip. But Stavrou had only worked on Marc's last album, 'Dandy In The Underworld', hardly a masterpiece – nor did it bear any resemblance to the magical production formula of his heyday.)

The single was the first to betray two of the band's major sources of inspiration: the cinema, and obsessions/fascinations dating from Sioux's childhood. 'The Staircase (Mystery)' took the horror out of one of the most alarming scenes in Hitchcock's *Psycho* and replaced it with a juvenile sense of awe. The original intention was that the flip-side would house 'Love In A Void', but Stavrou's presence provided the ideal opportunity to record their homage to their dear, departed glam idol.

Not surprisingly, having a major deal, a hit album, two successful singles and riding around in limousines meant it was time for the Siouxsie And The Banshees backlash, and the *NME*s Ian Penman was appointed executioner. Over the past few months, the band's self reverence had near enough burst its banks during interviews. Penman pulled the carpet from beneath them, and the idea that they existed in isolation as leaders of some 'anti-rock' vanguard quickly faded from this point on.

Accepting that the Banshee credo – slightly untoward subject matter, an undoubtedly fresh sound and a non-deferential attitude towards record companies – was unique to a point, he got behind the rhetoric to ensure no one would ever again mistake their game for anything other than rock 'n' roll. Whether a temporary 'blip' or not, to mention revolution and rock in the same breath today is laughable, but back in the late seventies idealism ran riot across the pages of both the underground and mainstream music press. To be tried and found guilty of counter-revolutionary practices was a heinous crime. Luckily for the band, few could ever make much sense of the debates which divided a nation's rock critics, and readers began to desert the weeklies – not The Banshees – in droves.

To the country's legion of Radio One listeners, Siouxsie's conversational style proved a shade too daring and after an appearance on *Roundtable* in May, she managed to get herself banned from live broadcasts. The programme centred on a pot-pourri of stars and DJs who would debate the week's latest single releases. She managed to wind up DJ Peter Powell to near-breaking point, so much so that at one point he could be heard complaining to the show's host Kid Jensen. Her unwillingness to submit to the show's usual anodyne style was hardly cricket. But it was her comments regarding marketing practices and over-zealous security guards at concerts – admittedly, two of rock music's most malignant cancers – that caused an upset.

Sioux: "It's up to the artist to have some sort of say in what's gonna happen to them."

Kid: "None of your singles have come from your album . . . "
Sioux: "No, I mean, that's proved disastrous. I mean, I thought that the public wanted, you know, variety and good value for money and all that shit, but it seems that they want to know the album before they get it and that means releasing every fucking track off the album."
Kid: "Ooops." (mumbles)
Sioux: "Oooh. Sorry!" (adopts BBC accent). "Very sorry."

After our obstreperous guest made mincemeat of Nick Lowe, disco music and Linda Ronstadt's legs, the subject turned to live concerts, in particular, The Banshees' recent charity show at the Rainbow which raised funds for handicapped children. It was the group's first UK appearance of the year, and was going well until the excitement of 'Hong Kong Garden' proved too much for those who felt the need to pull out a few rows of seats.

Consequently the cheque handed over to the National Society For Handi-capped Children was for a rather depleted sum of £3,026.93.

Kid: "You actually ended up promoting your own gigs in the early days . . ."
Sioux: "We still do. That's a thing that's been ignored. We still use Dave Woods and we don't use any of the big 'Mafia' type – Big People. We've been blacklisted by a lot of people because we don't do that."
Kid: "Why is that?"
Sioux: "We know Dave Woods and he knows us. It's really hard to control security at gigs, i.e. places like the Rainbow. We managed to control a certain amount of whether the bouncers are more violent than the audience or vice versa. Something weird happened at the Rainbow. We managed to control the security really well. They didn't interfere.

Siouxsie adopting BBC speak

"I've seen a lot of gigs where totally innocent people who've just stood up to appreciate a band have been dragged out of the fucking – sorry, sorry, wrong word – dragged out of the damned venue and beaten the hell out of. But in this instance, they had total freedom, yet the audience chose to take advantage of that and wrecked a lot of the seats that were there. Which is sad because you don't know what to do, whether you give them the freedom . . .

"It seems they need the antagonism of these security people which I hate. But I hate people getting hurt and hate the fact that we did a charity benefit and we had to pay something like two grand for the damages."

It was over two years before she was invited back to speak on BBC Radio.

The Siouxsie clones attended the Rainbow concert in droves. So did David Bowie but he retired to the bar mumbling something about the band being "too conservative." He'd recently been telling American radio listeners that Throbbing Gristle were the best thing happening in Britain: perhaps he failed to recognise that The Banshees were following his example in seeking to produce music which remained both innovative and accessible. "You have to maintain that line between the traditional and the unconventional all the time," Kenny once told Paul Morley. It was a sentiment that had oozed from every Bowie record since 'Space Oddity'.

Sounds magazine well understood the growing visual aspect of The Banshees' appeal and carried a two-page pictorial account of their promotional assault on Spain in April. This had been organised by Polydor, which was just as well, because the band's coffers were already being fast-depleted despite the bluff of the charity concert.

If the label hoped that the next 45 was going to be another 'Hong Kong Garden', they were wrong. 'Playground Twist', issued in June, was one of the most savage aural batterings ever to penetrate the usually placid waters of the top 30. It was released in the same week as Public Image Ltd's 'Death Disco' and for a brief moment it looked as if the 'New Music' was making major inroads into the mainstream. Both songs were loud, unrelenting, dirge-like mantras that most certainly signposted the way forward. The iconoclasts had triumphed: they had rebuilt a finely detuned rock machine that was a powerful affront to the soporific nightmare of top thirtydom.

Once again produced by Nils, with the help of Mike Stavrou, 'Playground Twist' was a swirling mass of flanged guitars, church bells, a massive drum sound and an anguished Banshee wail of a performance from Sioux. "If Ingmar Bergman produced records," wrote reviewer Roy Carr, "they would sound like this." But Bergman's intensity is delicate and understated; this record is a three-minute, frenzied kick in the face. On the promotional video, the band stand aloof and concentrated, but the austerity explodes into a grin as Sioux 'drowns' in a sea of urchins at the end. The flip, 'Pull To Bits', was built around a repeated bass line and featured washes of acoustic guitar and a not-entirely successful vocal from Sioux. The children's voices echoed 'The Kids' on Lou Reed's 1974 album, 'Berlin'.

Around the same time, a German-only release coupling 'Mittageisen' and 'Love In A Void' appeared in the shops as an expensive import. The A-side was a German-language version of 'Metal Postcard', recorded during sessions for the new album, while the flip featured a new version of 'Love In A Void'. Perhaps they felt this was a surreptitious way of making their old stage favourite available to their fans but, miffed at losing sales to their German counterparts, UK Polydor decided to release it in September. It didn't sell well and was treated more as a collector's release than a bid for success. Nevertheless, its release did call into question the amount of product control exercised by the band.

An item boasting John Heartfield artwork on the sleeve that was certainly unauthorised was the 'Love In A Void' bootleg which had begun to appear from under shop counters during the previous months. This full-length album featured both John Peel sessions plus three studio out-takes, 'Carcass', 'Make Up To Break Up' and 'Love In A Void'. The latter was a furious rendition with Sioux's heavily echoed vocals delivering the original lyric with playful exuberance; the version of 'Carcass' was obviously a run-through, while 'Make Up To Break Up' – good as it was – served to indicate just how far the band's songwriting had developed since 1977.

With the exception of a quietly mastered 'Carcass', the bootleg was of high quality and proved extremely popular with fans. One said: "Any Banshees fan would have felt really disappointed with that Polydor album as it's not nearly as good as 'Love In A Void'. I don't see why a real Banshees fan shouldn't have some memento of the reason they liked the band in the first place." The band were less impressed: "I don't mind if people just wanna tape stuff and have it for themselves," said Sioux the Fan. But Siouxsie the Singer was understandably aggrieved: "The reason we're in this company is so we can put out what we want out. And then someone who's not part of all this is just making money from what they wanna put out."

The front cover, featuring an early shot of Sioux in her bare-breasted 'window' T-shirt, and the inclusion of the original 'Love In A Void', gave the band additional grounds for complaint and proceedings were set in motion against the bootleggers. The record is now reputed to have sold 100,000 copies.

Anyone who'd seen the group at the Rainbow or heard their third John Peel session broadcast in April would have been exposed to several new songs that eventually appeared on 'Join Hands' in September. And despite Sioux's tirade against singles on albums in May, 'Playground Twist' ended up on it too. Early copies of the album featured a peel-off sticker with the ugly message: 'Contains their hit single, 'Playground Twist'.' So much for the much-lauded 'control' over their product! Perhaps that was the price they had to pay for spending three weeks in George Martin's plush AIR Studios situated along Oxford Street, at a cost of £30,000. And there was worse. Having dropped John Maybury's sleeve design concept which incorporated a picture of two small children getting married, because they couldn't trace the copyright owner, Nils hit upon the idea of having a plain cover embossed with four soldiers. But in the rush to get the album out in time for the tour announced for the autumn, no one stopped to order any proofs, and the sleeves returned with the soldiers printed rather than embossed. All the band could do was request a new label manager.

In concert in '78

The 'Join Hands' period was a difficult time. Arguments raged during its making; and its eventual release was over-shadowed by greater traumas within the Banshee camp. In many ways it is the band's forgotten album, only remembered for a lengthy and largely wasteful 13-minute version of 'The Lord's Prayer', and because it failed to branch out into the terrains suggested by 'Switch' or even 'Voices'. If 'The Lord's Prayer' is no more palatable today, time has been kinder to the rest of the record.

The overall sound was quite different to 'The Scream'. Though Nils Stevenson was executive producer, Mike Stavrou's hand held the controls, much against the wishes of John and Kenny. They would have been happier with the clarity and space achieved by Steve Lillywhite on the first LP. Nils later agreed Stavrou was a mistake. This initial dispute didn't help matters; neither did John's insistence that his songs weren't fully formulated. What the hell, there was always 'The Lord's Prayer' if they were really pushed!

Though the production had changed, it didn't alter the mood, but the unity that made 'The Scream' more than just a collection of songs was noticeably absent. 'Join Hands' was no less an anguished cry than its predecessor, its themes – the fallacy of community, faith and authority – no less pressing. Pity, then, that the project was hurried and unfinished.

The inspiration for 'Join Hands' weighed more heavily on external factors. The idea for 'Poppy Day', an evocation of the war graves in Flanders, came to Steve while watching the two-minute silence for the war dead on TV. Similarly, 'Regal Zone' was sparked off by a news item on the fighting in Iran; while the Middle East – which has proved a constant source of fascination for Sioux – cropped up again in the shape of a 'dervish spin' in 'Icon'. But the challenge of the social claustrophobia that was 'The Scream' had turned to morbid self pity on 'Premature Burial'.

The second side was a real mix of loose ends. It kicked off with 'Playground Twist' before shifting the mood radically for Sioux's elegiac 'Mother'. Then the material ran dry and the last 13-minutes or so was taken up with 'The Lord's Prayer'. Had time allowed, more could have been made of what seemed a totally arbitrary inclusion. After all, it had virtually disappeared from their live act since autumn 1978. Nils visualised it as a big production job – bring in an orchestra and choir, splice it up, maybe throw in some backward tapes. It could have been the band's answer to 'Revolution 9'. Unfortunately, the rest of the group thought the idea silly.

The Banshees have always taken great pride in lacing their apparently gothic sensibility with more than a hint of humour. The nearest 'Join Hands' got to that was the unwitting irony of the album title in the wake of subsequent developments. Steve disagreed: 'The Lord's Prayer' was, in his opinion, "a noisy joke. We're making this horrendous noise and Sioux's singing 'Clair De Lune'!" In actual fact it was turgid and uninspired, particularly when held up against its obvious precursor, The Velvet Underground's 'Sister Ray'. Game for a laugh, anyone?

Jon Savage wrote at the time, ''The songs are delivered with the stifling intensity of inner violence in a locked room.'' Whether he had inside information, acute perception or a crystal ball, he certainly knew which way the wind was blowing.

Crack

in the make-up

Part of the strength of Siouxsie And The Banshees was their apparent unity of purpose. Here were four highly motivated individuals, fortuitously bound by the clarion call for musical anarchy in 1976, and who had established a style and a sound unique enough already to inspire an army of imitators – both on and off stage. That July they had appeared at *ZigZag* magazine's 10th Anniversary Party to collect several Poll-Winners awards. They could have cleaned up had The Clash not pipped them in the Best LP, Best Group and Best Live Group categories. As it was 'The Staircase (Mystery)' won Best Single, Sioux walked off with Best Female Singer, and as she was far sexier and better dressed than Joe Strummer, she won those categories too. Unlike the majority of prima donnas present, the band at least had the decency to collect their awards, though roadie Les Mills had a simple message for the shysters: "You're all wankers!" he bellowed. But accolades were not enough. After two-and-a-half years working at a high level of intensity something had to snap. It couldn't have come at a worse moment.

The Defection (Mystery)

The 24-date UK autumn tour was just the first stage of a worldwide jaunt that would take in America, Canada, Japan and possibly Australia. After rehearsals at the Hammersmith Odeon, this major juncture in the band's development got under way with a couple of warm-up gigs in Bournemouth and Aylesbury. Neither went particularly well. They were only using half the PA and even that took a beating from Sioux on the second night as she responded angrily to the violence among the audience. Things hadn't improved in time for the tour's opening night at the Ulster Hall, Belfast, where a mix-up meant they had to borrow equipment in order to play the gig. It was rapidly degenerating into a farce.

The next date on what should have been called the 'Carry On Screaming' tour was in Aberdeen on September 7, but before the soundcheck, the band were booked for a promotional appearance at the Other Record Shop to sign copies of the new album and generally mingle with their fans. It was the first time The Banshees had condescended to an appearance of this kind and it ought to have been no more than a minor detail in their career. Instead, it marked a major turning point. It was the moment when drummer Kenny Morris and guitarist John McKay walked out.

The catalyst for their departure was the discovery that Nils had sold 30 promotional copies of 'Join Hands' to the shop owner, after it was discovered that only 50, instead of the required 250 copies had been sent by Polydor. Money changing hands for albums bearing 'Not For Sale' stickers was decidedly underhand for a band who had sought at every opportunity to expose the hypocrisy of the industry. John and Kenny refused to sign any and began giving copies away. They then replaced 'Join Hands' with the Slits' long-awaited 'Cut' album on the shop's turntable. (Later Sioux commented, "It must have been the tits and arse that attracted them," a reference to the cover depicting the three Slits covered in mud and makeshift loincloths.) Both shop and band manager were incensed. Sioux gave John a shove and he was gone, Kenny in tow. They returned to the hotel, hastily assembled pillow effigies of themselves, taking time to pin on their backstage passes, and ordered a taxi to Stonehaven some 15 miles down the coast. Along the way, they changed their plans and the taxi sped in the direction of the railway station. Nils caught up with them and tried to make some sense of the situation, but Kenny wound the window up on his hand uttering the immortal words, "We can't take the pressure."

Initially, Nils, Sioux and Steve assumed the pair had gone to cool off in the heat of the moment and expected them to appear at the soundcheck. Nils' and Steve's first reaction had been to caution Sioux for arguing in public. But when the manager returned from a brief encounter with the absconders, the truth became clear. The trio were absolutely shattered: "I just wouldn't want to live through that again," Severin recalled much later. "I've never had so much trauma in my life. It was horrible." One thing was certain, the defectors would only walk out on The Banshees once. A press release was hastily prepared: "Nils Stevenson and Pure Noise Limited wish to make it known that, as from Friday September 7, 1979, of their own volition, John Gareth McKay and Kenneth Ian Morris ceased to perform as members of the group professionally known as Siouxsie And The Banshees."

By the evening, the confusion had turned to venom. After a well-received set from Scottish hopefuls The Scars, and the tour's special guests The Cure, a voice came over the PA bringing the news most were half expecting: "Attention. Your attention please. Owing to the disappearance of two members of The Banshees, the gig will not take place. If you would stay in your seats, arrangements will be made to refund your money."

Kenny

Sioux and Steve then ambled on stage to fill in the detail: "Two original members of the band are here tonight. Two art college students fucked off out of it," said Sioux. "All I can say is we'll be back here with some friends who have got some roots. If you've got one per cent of the aggression we feel towards them, if you ever see them, you have my blessings to beat shit out of them. Next time you see them . . . pow!" Wham bam, thank you, Ma'am.

The Cure returned, played two more songs, then announced some special guests of their own. Sioux and Steve joined them for an old favourite: "John and Kenny were doing it for the money and you can't do a good 'Lord's Prayer' with that attitude," said the singer, "We'll be back!" Knowing they were party to something far more memorable than the gig they were expecting, the Scottish fans lapped it up. Round two to Sioux and Steve, born-again populists.

The music press were full of inquests in the weeks that followed. Sioux and Steve's version of the events were well publicised and hangers-on like *ZigZag*'s Kris Needs were called upon to back them up. And the knives really came out: "John is just utterly humourless, a dilettante who would never make a fool of himself. And Kenny was just into the group on a voyeuristic level, wanting to be part of a 'punk phenomenon' . . . I think that it is of paramount importance that you get across that they worked up a nice little marriage with each other and that they'd travel up their own arseholes with each other and console each other! That's when the trouble really started, when they became really, really fucked up." (Sioux)

"They were just pathetic. The band were growing apart. John and Kenny were going off into ga-ga land, totally abstract nonsense." (Nils)

John and Kenny, meanwhile, had gone into hiding. One early theory had them packed off to Paris for a rendezvous with PiL or even The Psychedelic Furs (managed by ex-Banshees roadie Les Mills). Wherever they were, only one person in the Banshee camp received any communication – their bodyguard: "They phoned him to apologise and said that he was the last one they wanted to hurt, knowing full well that if anyone could kill them it would be him," sneered Steve.

After the dust had been allowed to settle, John and Kenny broke their two-month silence by circulating a letter among the music weeklies. While Nils Stevenson was allowed several column inches to tear each point apart, it still remains an essential document in terms of the band's motivations, the validity of what they were selling and the real nature of the business in which Siouxsie And The Banshees had got involved.

The bottom line is usually money. When Kenny and John walked out, Nils pleaded with them that much of the group's finances were tied up in the tour. (Around £50,000 had been invested in the tour. Some of this was put up by Dave Woods, but the bulk came from the band's earnings. Each cancelled venue would mean a lost deposit of around £5,000.) This fell on deaf ears as the window of the departing taxi wound higher and higher. Both John and Kenny knew that their defection could prove financially damaging, and even today, the case slapped on them to recover lost monies remains unresolved. With this in mind, the split was undoubtedly the result of an ideological dispute, as the elopers were prepared to put their money where their mouths were.

and John on the way out

They wrote: ''If any one member felt that the trust and communication fundamental to a performance was missing, then that person should not go on-stage or persist in upholding any such false situation. This basic honesty was and is vital, and it is a testament to just how much is remembered of those early ideals, that no one even hinted at that as a possible reason for our departure. The incident at the record shop just served as a catalyst and tipped the already finely balanced scales towards the spur of the moment decision.

''Another of these unwritten principles was that we would use commercialism to our advantage, without poisoning and misdirecting any of the original energy and ideals into the financial treadmill of album, tour, single and all its inherent limitations. Siouxsie and Steve believed in the direction that the management was steering us, while we felt that we were getting dangerously close to the brand of commercialism which we had all held out for two years to avoid.

''Over the period of time which elapsed between 'The Scream' and 'Join Hands', the emphasis shifted from what we as a unit wanted, to what we as a unit ought to do to retain our tenuous grip on commercial success.''

They continued by bemoaning Nils' desire to 'cash in' on the band's success, how the power struggles led to ''a unity of three against two'' and how The Banshees' bid to expand musically was thwarted by the lack of a permanent rehearsal room. It ended with John asking for the return of his guitar, which had been given away by Nils at the Aberdeen gig with the words, ''We won't be needing this any more.'' Had the walk-out been wholly premeditated, McKay would have probably taken his guitar with him.

There is no doubting the fact that John and Kenny had discussed the possibility of leaving. McKay had already had discussions with his solicitor in order to clarify his legal position within the band. Though tensions within the group had existed as far back as the making of 'The Scream', they were argued out face to face. But by the time of 'Join Hands', the pair had begun to show a distinct disinterest in the product. As well as being a hurried album, John's solo guitar piece 'Infantry' was left off, while the time-consuming joke 'The Lord's Prayer' which it should have followed remained intact. Disappointed with the sound on 'Join Hands', he wanted Steve Lillywhite reinstated to handle the band's production. Before this, a major disagreement had occurred over 'The Staircase (Mystery)' sleeve, which John and Kenny hated.

Increasingly, it seems, important decisions went against them. According to Steve, things came to a head before the tour, but both pledged ''one hundred per cent commitment.'' If the acrimonious split was a spur of the moment thing, then it was also an inevitable result of the gradual escalation of tension. Later, in December, at a party held for Blondie at the Notre

Dame Hall, Leicester Square, Sioux and Steve spotted Kenny and laid into him with stilettos and fists. "He was a fool to think, just because it was Christmas, that nothing would happen. They're forgotten, but not forgiven. The whole affair still leaves me cold," said Sioux.

A catastrophe concentrates the mind wonderfully, and with The Banshees in tatters, the ideological concerns which meant so much in the past were largely forgotten. The immediate problem was how to salvage something from a tour they had barely started. And somehow they had to reconstruct a new-look band. There was no way that two strong-willed individuals like Sioux and Steve were going to let the deserters have the last laugh. Though the next five dates were cancelled they were adamant the tour would go on. Sioux had told the Aberdeen audience that they'd be back with some old friends and, within hours, rumours of Marco Pirroni (at a loose end before plotting Antmania with Adam) and those ex-Pistols Paul Cook and Steve Jones, abounded. After the weekend, Severin told reporters that neither was a realistic proposition, but that rehearsals were going ahead in London to find replacement members.

Though Paul Cook declined the offer, he suggested they contact Budgie, whose most recent recorded work had been – ironically – for The Slits' 'Cut' album. After just a day's rehearsal he was in. John Peel broadcast nightly SOS's on his show, but after two days of auditions, none of the guitar hopefuls could fit the bill. Marco got further than Cook or Jones, but it was 1976 all over again – he just wasn't right. Finally Cure guitarist Robert Smith was persuaded to stand in, even though it meant playing two sets a night. After only six days of rehearsals, the 'Join Hands' tour reconvened at the De Montfort Hall, Leicester, less than two weeks after the walk-out.

A new mood permeated The Banshees' camp. Smith got the band into bad habits, though the long nights of merry-making helped wash away earlier problems – and blot out some scrappy performances turned in by the makeshift outfit! "Isn't it great not to have a pair of old women moaning away in the corner," enthused Sioux. Even the band's intransigent stage persona melted as Smith and Budgie exchanged grins each time one of them forgot his cue. Although a decision regarding permanent members would be made after the tour, Sioux and Steve had discussed the possibility of keeping The Banshees as a loose aggregation, recruiting musicians to suit the songs: "I see it as being the one sure way of staying fresh, of destroying the idea of a group as a marriage," said the bassist.

Perhaps it was the combination of delayed shock and too many late nights, but whatever the reason, illness plagued Sioux throughout the tour causing a spate of further cancellations. On October 3, she was taken ill after a concert in Newcastle, and rushed to hospital with suspected laryngitis. After discharging herself prematurely to continue the tour, she managed the final southern round of dates climaxing with a performance at London's

Hammersmith Odeon – and then collapsed while celebrating the end of the tour with friends and relatives. This time, stomach and throat pains were diagnosed as 'hepatitis and ancillary ailments', and she was ordered to take two months' rest. Sioux put this convalescence period to good use by learning some basic guitar and writing a dozen songs. A proposed November US mini-tour lined up for them by Miles Copeland was out of the question, but they did manage one other public appearance that year, playing 'Love In A Void' and 'Regal Zone' on BBC's *Something Else*.

Budgie and Steve in 1980

And Then
There Were
Three

In December, Nils surprised no one when he announced that Budgie was to remain a Banshee. As for a guitarist, the band hedged their bets: ''We're taking our time and waiting for the right person.'' Robert Smith was happy playing with The Banshees on tour, but for the time being, preferred to retain his independence. Instead he asserted his new-found confidence within The Cure and promptly sacked Michael Dempsey.

Budgie's recruitment gave the pair a vital lift and helped restore some of their confidence. As well as rejoicing in a curious nickname (stemming from his childhood passion for the bird), the boy who was once just plain old Peter Clark was regarded as one of the finest sticksmen to have emerged from the DIY era. In just two years, he'd already paid his dues in a variety of Liverpool combos: The Opium Eaters, The Nova Mob, The Spitfire Boys and Big In Japan. The St. Helens-born, Liverpool Polytechnic student was also a popular figure on the scene and had a regular spot DJ'ing at Eric's Club, which was the hub of the Mersey scene.

After making the move to London in search of session work, he found himself as a temporary replacement for the departing Palmolive in the all-girl band, The Slits. After adding a distinctly dub-wise drum sound on the 'Cut' LP, this nine-month stint ended in the summer of 1979 when he joined ex-Pistol Glen Matlock's aborted supergroup, Jimmy Norton's Explosion. This hadn't long folded before Paul Cook recommended him to Nils.

During December, The Banshees trio auditioned dozens of possible guitarists. Most had learnt their repertoire from 'The Scream' and 'Join Hands', but the acid test came with the new material, where few showed any signs of originality. Sioux recalled this frustrating scenario to Kris Needs: "We got so bored with trying the old Banshees' songs on people, 'cos they just had to do their homework and maybe they could do it, but it wasn't good enough to say yes to. But we got bored with them anyway. There were a lot of boring guitarists so we just started writing things on the spot in the rehearsal to see if they could join in and add something of their own." The band ended up with several new songs, but still no guitarist.

Nils told the press: "There are three hopefuls at the moment, but nothing has been decided. They know which song they want for the single, but things haven't worked out properly yet." Steve Jones dropped in for a seasonal jam session for a couple of days, but running through old Pistols' songs like 'Bodies' was hardly a serious audition.

The band were really killing time waiting for John McGeoch, guitarist and key songwriter for Magazine, to return from America. Though a founder member of the outfit formed by one-time Buzzcock Howard Devoto, John was sufficiently interested enough to journey down to London to meet the band: "When I heard that Sioux and Steve wanted to work with me, I was flattered. I loved 'The Scream' when I heard it; I knew they were pursuing something of interest. I went down to meet them for the first time round about Christmas in Notting Hill. Steve Strange told me to wear black if I wanted to make the right impression. We had a meal and got drunk, and that was it, we got along."

By the end of a weekend's rehearsal, this new aggregation had three songs fully worked out, 'Desert Kisses', 'Drop Dead' and 'Happy House'. But McGeoch was unwilling to leave Magazine at this stage, particularly as they were about to begin work on 'The Correct Use Of Soap' album. An arrangement was reached whereby he would be employed on a temporary basis and paid a standard session fee for his work. This suited John who was on the look out to increase his extra-curricular activities anyway.

John McGeoch lining up with Sioux, Steve and Budgie

"It was a standard joke about 'going psychedelic' but some good things came from that period. We used 'Arnold Layne' and The Stones' 'Satanic Majesties' as influences." (Steve)

She Comes
In Colours
Everywhere

The first fruits of the new arrangement came with the 'Happy House' single in March 1980. This was quite clearly a different animal than before yet still managed to sound like a Siouxsie And The Banshees record. It was a trick the band would repeat again and again. If the themes of madness and childhood established continuity, the sound was lighter and less urgent than before. The bass was far more prominent, Budgie seduced subtle innuendos from his kit instead of trying to murder it, while McGeoch weaved in and out with fluid, mysterious guitar lines heavily bathed in echo.

But Morris and McKay weren't forgotten. The flip, 'Drop Dead/ Celebration' was a gut-wrenching affair so filled with venom that the words were almost indecipherable. "I suppose it was inspired by them," commented Sioux, "but then you can look at a turd in the street and be inspired to write a song about it." Any doubt was allayed by the etched message in the run-off groove: 'Bye Bye Blackheads'. The song doubles as pastiche (with its inverted 'Jigsaw Feeling' riff) and purification, but if they thought this would purge them of the pair, then they were wrong.

There was still some unfinished business of the cancelled dates from the previous tour and McGeoch was persuaded to join the band for seven Scottish dates plus two nights at London's Music Machine. Of all places, it kicked off with a warm-up date in Magazine's home town of Manchester.

Among the new songs featured were 'Hybrid', 'Desert Kisses' and 'Christine', the latter already being touted as a follow-up to 'Happy House'.

When McGeoch left for a spring tour with Magazine, The Banshees faced a difficult decision whether to share a guitarist with another name band or find a more permanent replacement. The decision was made for them in April when John announced he was quitting Magazine to pursue a variety of solo projects. Apart from moonlighting as a Banshee he was a member of Steve Strange's pick-up band Visage. Also lined up was session work with Generation X and production chores with Belgian group De Kreuners; recently, he'd stood in for a flu-ridden Stuart Adamson on a Skids session recorded for John Peel (which also featured Steve on backing vocals). Though legal difficulties prevented John from calling himself a Banshee he was, for all intents and purposes, the band's fourth member.

Now that the group's sound had undergone a remarkable transformation on 'Happy House', this was utilised to much greater effect on 'Christine', which harked back to the moodiness of the earlier material. Though traces of Charles Manson, children's TV, R.D. Laing, and disaster news stories had inhabited the band's early work, it was the infamous schizophrenic Christine Sizemore who became the first of The Banshees' great obsessions. Steve learnt of her in a Sunday colour supplement a couple of years earlier and became intrigued by this American woman with 22 identifiable personalities. Each one had a name and several were put to good use on the song: Strawberry Girl, Banana Split Lady, Turtle Lady and Purple Lady.

Once again, the B-side featured the more typical material, and 'Eve White/ Eve Black' proved that the old bite had far from deserted them. As with 'Drop Dead', it had been produced without the assistance of Nigel Gray (fresh from working with The Police, and recommended by McGeoch), who delicately handled the A-sides. One reviewer wrote that the song was The Banshees' version of Pink Floyd's 'Careful With That Axe, Eugene' and he wasn't far wrong. Both share an opening air of quiet unease, pierced by a blood-curdling scream that acts as a cue for a full-blast aural assault. Unsurprisingly, it remained a stage favourite for several years.

Neither B-side appeared on the long-awaited 'Kaleidoscope' album when it finally appeared in August. But both singles were strategically poised at the start of each side in the hope of tempting the customers. Many were disappointed: 'Kaleidoscope' proved an expensive method of purchasing two top 30 hits. In spite of the title, with its connotations of adventure and endless variety, 'Kaleidoscope' offered far less than it promised. It may have derived some sort of cohesion from its very fragmentation but neither Sioux or Steve were consistent songwriters and some of the material was distinctly third-rate. As for the precocious experiments with synthesisers, Sioux had called her own bluff on *Roundtable* a year earlier when she said such a recourse was an excuse for laziness and a lack of originality.

The album did have its moments, particularly 'Desert Kisses', a love song that remains one of the band's most deliciously out of character recordings. Another highlight was 'Skin', a rousing venture into social comment sung with all the scathing attack of a vegetarian – except that Sioux wasn't one yet! If guest guitarist Steve Jones sounded uninspired on 'Clockface', and perfunctory on 'Paradise Place', here he provided the perfect foil for Budgie's butcher's knife drum rolls.

Sioux playing occasional guitar

'Kaleidoscope' may not have established any real parameters for future possibilities, but it gave the group a breathing space. Though the musical progress was awkward, their fraternisations with the new rock élite met with more success. McGeoch, and to a lesser extent Robert Smith, had liberated them from an insular life where they wouldn't even show their faces on a record sleeve. In London, they joined faces-about-town like Richard Jobson, while Sioux did the rounds in the States, dining with Iggy Pop and bumping noses with the likes of Devo, Debbie Harry, and old friends Phil Oakey and Johnny Thunders.

Having taken time to relax and muse over the mixed reception that greeted 'Kaleidoscope', Siouxsie And The Banshees prepared for their longest concert tour yet. This began with three low-key dates at the start of September billed as Janet And The Icebergs – a reference to the cold warrior image which prevailed among press and fans. Days later, they topped the bill at the second Futurama Festival held at Queen's Hall, Leeds. Like most events where sheer numbers grossly outweigh facilities, it was a miserable affair, but at least Steve didn't set his bass amp alight as he'd done a few nights earlier in Liverpool. The sight of Sioux striking a few guitar chords on 'Paradise Place' was one of the choice moments when excerpts from the festival were broadcast on TV. Also shown was an edited version of 'Eve White/Eve Black'. Rumours that Robert Fripp (the ex-King Crimson guitarist who'd worked with Bowie in recent years) would join the band onstage proved unfounded. The Banshees weren't ready for blowing sessions just yet. One new song was aired during the dates; a primitive version of 'Voodoo Dolly'.

The whole of October and November was spent on the road, two weeks on the Continent, two in Britain and a month in the States. Having taken the somewhat surprising step of establishing a fan club earlier in the year (at one stage, it was going to be called 'Happy House', though they settled for 'The File'), Sioux then took the opportunity in interviews to express some reservations about the whole fan/star set-up: "I've never in my life asked for an autograph. I never wanted that. I never wanted to wait outside a gig to touch Marc Bolan or whatever. I never wanted to find out where they were living. I just didn't want that. I was just thrilled when a new single came out, or when there was a new photo in the paper.

"I'm not surprised that people buy the records, but I am surprised by the way it's still treated as a big deal to see Siouxsie going into a hotel, or trying to get backstage to find me . . . all this surprises me. I thought it would change but it hasn't. I feel I must let a lot of people down 'cos I don't do all the clichés that you associate with pop stars."

It's a difficult subject, though Sioux's uni-dimensional perception of the 'fan' as the poor, passive relation belies the two-way nature of the system. This deity/supplicant role-play only lasts as long as the fan wants it to. There always comes a time when they 'drain' their idol and move on. Ask Adam Ant.

As for the ghoulish array of lookalikes which seemed to double in number on every tour, was she flattered? "No. I should be impressed but I'm not. I just wish people had more pride in themselves and thought more of themselves. I switch off." Nevertheless, Steve and Sioux were sufficiently impressed with a tape sent to them by a group of Scottish Banshee plagiarists called Altered Images to offer them a support slot on the British leg of the tour. Steve ended up producing their first couple of singles.

Considering The Banshees had no current deal in the States ('Join Hands' was turned down by Geffen who had issued 'The Scream'), their winter series of US club dates was quite a success, even if they'd stuck to cities where there was a relatively large minority of new wave fanatics. They ended the year with a sell-out performance at the Hammersmith Palais where they played several new songs: 'Israel', 'Red Over White', 'Into The Light' and 'Congo Conga'. Steve, together with Richard Jobson and 'The File' organiser Billy Houlston saw in the New Year by gate-crashing the stage during an Altered Images performance at the Moonlight . From hell in Aberdeen to Hogmanay in Hampstead. At least they could smile now.

"Following the footsteps of a rag doll dance we are entranced spellbound."

Altered images can be deceptive. Colourful Japanese robes and nights on the town with the rock nobility convinced no one that The Banshees weren't sliding further into a gothic quagmire. Their old image returned to haunt them with a vengeance but throughout 1981 they were too busy touring to be able to afford a major rethink of the Banshee milieu. Perhaps playing to concert halls full of creatures from the black lagoon night after night had finally got the better of them.

Their New Year got off to an early start with the release of 'Israel' at the end

lory

of November 1980. Marking a return to the self-assuredness perfected by the band of old, the single was the first (disregarding 'Mittageisen', which wasn't really new product) not to reach the top 40. In retrospect, they have always regretted recording the song while still in its embryonic stages, and particularly not making enough of the choir buried way down in the mix. But 'Israel' has since become something of an anthem, a testament to endurance, not just of the state it eulogises, but of the band which, too, has continued to flourish in an often adverse climate. Steve Severin wouldn't argue. When asked whether 'Israel' was a political song, he said no. "It's more general. (It could represent) a disillusioned person or a whole race who've ceased to understand or believe in what they held to be the truth." Few turn blood into wine as well as Siouxsie And The Banshees.

The song was written on tour, bits were added just prior to performing it on BBC's *Something Else*, and it was recorded on Guy Fawkes' Night so that it could be climbing the charts by the time the band returned from the States. Being their first single also released on 12-inch made its relative failure all the more surprising. Those investing in the latter were disappointed to find bogus timings on the label, but what once looked like a rip-off now attracts a healthy price on the collector's market.

The single brought with it another symbol, the Star of David, which appeared on its sleeve, labels, promotional posters and T-shirts. The latter came in handy when a sieg-heiling group of skinheads disrupted a gig in Derby: the band walked off the stage and returned minutes later wearing the shirts. For those who weren't aware of the significance the band launched into 'Drop Dead' to ensure that the message came across loud and clear.

Having played 24 gigs during the last quarter of 1980, The Banshees felt sufficiently confident to begin their 12-date New Year tour with a couple of concerts at the Hammersmith Odeon. Once, sheets of cold blue and white lights lit the band: for the Join Hands Tour, a church backdrop hung behind them, adding a hallowed tone to their sermons. But now that stage presentation had been reinstated as an acceptable part of live performance, the group quickly utilised this dimension for additional effect. ''When we play now,'' Budgie admitted, ''it's a show and not a gig. The lights now are brilliant.'' During 'Israel', a skyline of clouds appeared on a backscreen; 'Red Light' was suitably lit, complete with strobe flashes to accompany the sound of a camera's autowind; and the band's new pièce de résistance, 'Night Shift', incorporated lightning flashes of electricity to heighten its impact. It provided a chilling moment.

The tour ended at Warwick University where the concert was recorded for the BBC's *Rock Goes To College* series. Sioux's untrained singing voice wasn't up to the punishing schedule the group had followed since last autumn and the cracks were beginning to show. This would prove a greater problem in the months ahead.

We Put Our Magic On You

By 1981 Siouxsie And The Banshees had risen to the top of the Class of '77. The Buzzcocks had gone off the boil and split, The Damned kept coming and going like a recurring pain in the head, PiL emigrated to New York thinking they'd discovered video when instead it turned out to be lager and fast food in front of a TV set, and The Clash were simply an embarrassment. At the same time an ongoing battle raged regarding the true inheritors of the 'punk' tradition. Unsurprisingly, the easily aped Sham/Angelic Upstarts/UK Subs wing came out on top, and spawned a comic-strip generation of mohican-headed, stud-covered punks beloved by London sightseers. Anyone able to read the back of a leather jacket knew the new names of the 'new' punk combos: Flux Of Pink Indians, Discharge, Subhumans, Chron Gen, The Exploited.

Such was the strength of The Banshees' sound and image that, to many eyes, they remained the one credible link with an increasingly mythical past. Having beaten off record company disinterest and a painful split in full view of the public they were determined to continue. Desperately needing the musical back-up to reassert their primacy, the band invoked 'Juju'.

The most important thing about 'Juju' was that it showed Siouxsie And The Banshees functioning as a band again. McGeoch had now been granted official status, but while he carried much of the songwriting burden in the way McKay had done, Sioux and Steve retained the reins over the lyrical and conceptual direction. It was an appropriate partnership. The resonance of the song titles said as much about the music as any critic could: 'Voodoo Dolly', 'Night Shift', 'Spellbound', 'Sin In My Heart', 'Halloween', 'Into The Light', 'Arabian Knights' and 'Head Cut'. "It's getting back to the actual name, drawing from images we had in mind when we first decided to call the band Siouxsie And The Banshees," said Steve.

Producer Nigel Gray managed to get his 'Walking On The Moon' guitar sound on to 'Into The Light' but each incantation to superstition and fascination was covered in a thick fog by the mixing desk. Even the pop brilliance of 'Spellbound' and 'Arabian Knights' was painted a shade too grey though this didn't halt their chart ascent. The accompanying videos, all enchanted forests, sword fights and flying carpets, were crass, gaudy and obviously served to provide a lighter moment after several weeks in the studio. Either that or someone thought he was Alexander Korda.

While both singles boasted a 12-inch counterpart, a distinctly irritating pattern was beginning to emerge. No one could complain about the regular inclusion of a bonus track even if they all sounded like lesser out-takes from LP sessions. But why they had to keep spoiling the A-sides by adding short bursts of instrumental passages was beyond comprehension. It may have added an extra minute or so to the song but served only to disrupt the flow of a finely-balanced piece of music.

A couple of days before their 'Juju' was unleashed on the public, executives at BBC Radio felt confident enough to invite Sioux back for a live, on-air appearance on Richard Skinner's mid-evening show. This was not due to any liberalisation of the airwaves; merely that Sioux was better house-trained now. (A few months later, in a retrospective on The Sex Pistols, the weekly scandal sheet *News Of The World* described the modern Sioux thus: "Now she tries to pretend she's a very good girl, throwing very suburban Sunday lunch parties where everyone says 'Pass the mint sauce'!")

Four songs specially recorded for the show were broadcast, including relaxed versions of 'Arabian Knights' and 'Head Cut' from the album, plus a couple of tracks that had appeared on B-sides. 'Red Over White' had altered significantly since its début on the flip of 'Israel', but the godawful cover of Ben E. King's 'Supernatural Thing' was no improvement on the one which accompanied 'Arabian Knights'. Sioux tried her best – after all, it had been her idea to record it – but the lack of enthusiasm shown by the rest was evident. Someone should have told them then to leave the whole field of cover versions to their lesser contemporaries – before it got out of hand.

Sioux enthused about the current band to the Radio One DJ and promptly whisked it off for an extensive one-month European jaunt. But not before announcing another lengthy series of UK dates which would take them through to the start of September, along with the rider that this may be The Last Time. It was a mark of the success of both 'Juju' and the singles from it that the faithful attended in their droves and finally convinced the band that their British base was well and truly established. Over the next 12 months they would concentrate their efforts elsewhere with return visits to America and the Continent and maiden tours of the Far East and Scandinavia.

Though the band's stage show had become more of a spectacle than ever before, the reaction to it confused Sioux: "This is the first time we're not fighting something in the audience, and it's an odd twist that we should end up fighting the adulation."

'We are Entranced Entranced Entranced Entranced Entranced Entranced.'

Steve had different ideas for the future: "I used to go down Cabaret Futura and that's what convinced me that touring is getting to be irrelevant. What Richard Strange has done is one idea that's partly worked. The most obvious next step for us would be Wembley or something, but we've never wanted to do it. Now's the time to stop and think how we want to do things."

If he only had the time. The only nod in the direction of Strange's mixed media presentation was to precede their show with a film of Alfred Jarry's 'Ubu Roi'. But without the eye-slitting sequence which made the presentation of the Dali/Bunuel collaboration, *Un Chien Andalou*, such a success at Bowie's 1976 Thin White Duke concerts, audiences remained spellbound by the drinks at the bar.

Steve and John had a unique opportunity to experience the band as part of the audience when Sioux and Budgie performed two songs, 'So Unreal' and 'But Not Them', written during the 'Juju' recording sessions in the spring. What they knew – and the audience did not – was that Sioux and Budgie had recorded an EP's worth of material in three days before the tour which they wanted released.

"No, seriously, we're just friends." (Sioux)

The Creatures was Steve's suggestion but the sleeve was a whim of Sioux and Budgie's. They had toyed with the idea of being photo- **Animal** graphed on Hamburg's notorious, sailor-infested Reeperbahn, but settled for a semi-nude shower scene in a Newcastle hotel. Well it certainly made a change from discussing the futility of the burgeoning Batcave scene and how their audiences had let them **Capers** down. "We wanted it to be close," said the Mad-Eyed Screamer, "not like Dollar or anything; to be sensual and yet funny. We tried to shock and amuse at the same time." And romance? "We're in love! And I'm in love with Steve and I'm in love with John." "And I'm in love with them all," chirped Budgie. What the pictures did confirm was Sioux's love for the erotic imagery of surrealist photographer Man Ray.

The notorious shower scene

After problems over the legal definition of a single and an LP, the pair were spared the trauma of dropping a song and the five-track 'Wild Things' EP was released in September in the form of two 45's. It fared no worse than any recent Banshee single by stalling at number 24. Nothing on it suggested a direction that was particularly stunning or original, but the pared down sound was a refreshing contrast to the satanic majesty of 'Juju'. And if Sioux was leaving false scents she did a good job on the title track, a cover of The Troggs' 'Wild Thing', the song that made such an impact on a nine-year-old girl from Chislehurst,

In Newcastle, where Sioux and Budgie were photographed by Adrian Boot "wet, exhausted and pissed," The Banshees played a concert for participants of the three day Handicapped Olympics at the Centre Hotel. "Us old spastics with two legs, two arms and two eyes are gonna play for them," said Sioux, without a hint of condescension. It proved to be one of their most memorable gigs. The band played waltz versions of songs like 'The Staircase (Mystery)' while the far from passive audience displayed their own talents by wheelchair dancing.

Before leaving for their second US tour, a new single 'Fireworks' was recorded, with a release date planned for Bonfire Night. But the rushed efforts proved unsatisfactory and it was postponed until it could be taped properly in the New Year.

Instead, a compilation of the band's singles was prepared for release in time for the Christmas market, and sales were helped along with the support of a major advertising campaign by Polydor. Not only that, the Banshee cognoscenti who snap up every record as soon as it's released, received a limited edition colour print of Sioux. Though a couple of rumours surrounded the album – one, that Polydor had planned to call it 'From The Beginning' and wanted to give it a cartoon sleeve featuring Sioux in a cot; the other, that early copies would come with a bonus seven-inch of unreleased material – it was a straightforward documentation of the band's single releases, spiced up with the inclusion of a slightly different mix of 'Love In A Void' and the inevitable 'Mirage'. This compilation, titled 'Once Upon A Time', outsold 'The Scream' and remains the band's biggest selling album. It also appeared as a video though a lack of promo films for both 'Mirage' and 'Love In A Void' meant they were replaced by 'Red Light'.

Its success came at a good time because the group had been negotiating a new deal with Polydor. Once this had been settled, their long-time manager and biggest fan, Nils Stevenson, decided to quit. Later he teamed up again with his old mentor Malcolm McLaren. Agent Dave Woods was the logical successor and took over on the eve of the group's six-date tour of Hong Kong and Japan (financed with the help of a sponsorship deal with Yamaha). Sioux was already prepared for the trip. A month earlier, in February, she'd been pictured on the cover of *The Face* dressed in full Japanese chic.

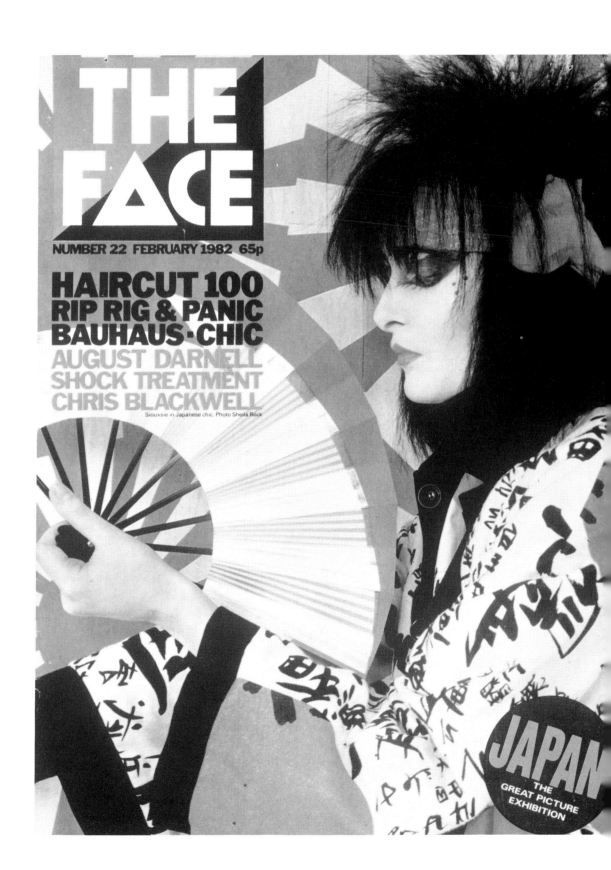

THE F∆CE

NUMBER 22 FEBRUARY 1982 65p

HAIRCUT 100
RIP RIG & PANIC
BAUHAUS·CHIC
AUGUST DARNELL
SHOCK TREATMENT
CHRIS BLACKWELL

Siouxsie in Japanese chic. Photo Sheila Rock

JAPAN
THE GREAT PICTURE EXHIBITION

It was far more appropriate than the 250,000 dollars-worth of mink and leather she wore for *Soho News* while in the US. On their return from the East, Sioux showed a fondness for a less ostentatious peaked cap which made several appearances, most notably on an *NME* front cover where she wore little else.

After the internal upheavals and Far East tour, the band's long-awaited single arrived in April, and they made an appearance on *Top Of The Pops* where Sioux modelled a couple of dead starlings hanging from her ears. The opening bars of orchestra made it obvious they had moved on from what was near self-parody on the previous year's 'Juju'. 'Fireworks' was unique for the mechanised eighties in that it boasted real strings – scored from a McGeoch guitar part by ex-Ravishing Beauty, Virginia Astley – and not a synthetic imitation: "They give it a real, earthy rich sound," explained Sioux. "You could hear the strings splitting and breathing and wheezing. Me and Steve have always wanted our music to be performed by the Royal Philharmonic Orchestra." If they did, they'd been keeping it very quiet!

Martin Rushent, who'd produced a string of hits for The Buzzcocks and was by now masterminding Altered Images' bid for pop stardom (taking over from where Steve left off), had been pencilled in to work on 'Fireworks' but found himself overbooked. Instead, the group produced it themselves with the assistance of engineer Mike Hedges, who'd previously worked with The Cure and The Associates. Before travelling to Scandinavia, The Banshees recorded several new songs with him, including 'Cascade' and 'Painted Bird'.

Too Many Quacks For My Liking

It was just as well that some material for the new album had already been recorded, as Sioux's recurrent throat problem took a turn for the worse during the tour. The cold weather wasn't entirely to blame as John McGeoch made clear: "We've virtually been on a world tour for the past year, and on every part of it, Sioux came down with something that local doctors would prescribe as laryngitis."

Anyone who caught the 1981 Nottingham concert shown on LWT a few months earlier would have heard her throat cracking badly. John was the only one to escape illness, but while Budgie and Steve's colds soon passed, Sioux was in bad shape. On June 12, the British music press printed reports that she'd been told to rest her voice until 1983. Even worse was the news that her singing style would have to be drastically altered or she'd have to give up completely.

As it turned out, the advice of Dr Sanner, one of Europe's leading throat specialists, was over-dramatised. After cancelling several Scandinavian dates Sioux got a second opinion from a London expert who was far less alarmist. Their first British date of the year, at the Elephant Fayre festival

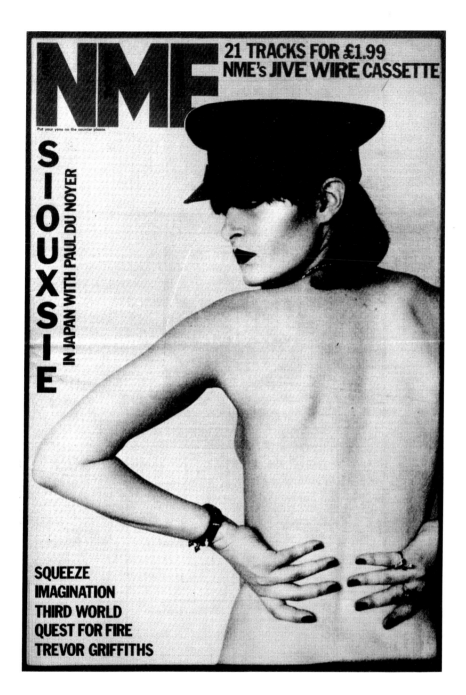

NME

**21 TRACKS FOR £1.99
NME's JIVE WIRE CASSETTE**

Put your yens on the counter please.

SIOUXSIE

IN JAPAN WITH PAUL DU NOYER

**SQUEEZE
IMAGINATION
THIRD WORLD
QUEST FOR FIRE
TREVOR GRIFFITHS**

scheduled for July, could go ahead. It seems that singers can develop a second set of vocal chords and it turned out to be those which were damaged; but to avoid the Joe Cocker syndrome, she was nevertheless ordered to rest as much as possible, stop drinking and smoking and have regular check-ups with her doctor.

If only it was so simple: "She treats every doctor as a quack," complained Steve. "Sioux is so stubborn that I can't believe she (won't) stop singing for six months." Sioux's verdict: "Doctors make you iller than you are."

Over the past few months, there had been a new pop boom which saw the likes of Altered Images, Human League and New Order making inroads into the UK charts. The band had hoped to capitalise on this. Not that Sioux had much time for the current state of pop: "It's depressingly safe and shallow and completely disposable. People are so insecure that they're playing music that's boring, music that has no sex or aggression or emotion. Present pop is all calculated, it lacks the emotions and the lunacy of the pop of the sixties."

And if she had a magic wand? "I'd love to see a *Top Of The Pops* with us, The Birthday Party, The Cramps and Suicide. That's how exciting I remember *Ready Steady Go!* as being." Some hope. It was over another year before The Banshees managed to crack the top 30, though they did share a hit at the same time as their old friends Public Image Ltd.

At the Elephant Fayre on July 31, the band's first UK outdoor gig, almost 50 per cent of the 16-song set consisted of new material. They had hoped to arrange a second open-air event in London later in the summer but were met with restrictions and regulations laid down by the GLC and Park Commissionaires. Instead, they returned to the studio to finish off the new album announced in mid-August as 'A Kiss In The Dreamhouse'. Its title derived from an unusual slant to the star system as Sioux explained: "Steve came up with the title while watching TV one night. A series was starting based around the twenties or thirties and this top-class whorehouse in America. In the whorehouse you could meet perfect replicas of the stars of the time, women like Mae West, perfectly reproduced. It was a very rich and exclusive place and it actually existed."

'A Kiss In The Dreamhouse' remained Sioux and Steve's favourite Banshees' album until the release of 1988's 'Peepshow'. Shimmering tales of passion and desire displaced the more stolid excursions into magic and superstition on 'Juju'.

One important difference between the two albums was that the material on 'Dreamhouse' was given space to evolve in the studio, whereas most of 'Juju' had been played into the ground before it was recorded. To the fore were the accoutrements; not just the obvious additions like the strings on 'Slowdive' and 'Obsession', but bells, tambourines, recorders, tape loops and delicate guitar touches. The top heavy power chords and full drum sound which characterised the traditional 'Banshees' sound had been pulled out of the mix to make room for this new textural emphasis – and it worked. Of course the mere hint of an acoustic guitar was enough to send many a rock scribe in search of the correct spelling of hippie. Even cranks like Nick Lowe saw fit to pass judgement: he called The Banshees' music "boring sub-hippie drivel dressed up in knickers for the sake of art."

'Cascade' never made it as a single but 'Slowdive' and the sublime 'Melt!' did. Sadly, neither broached the top 40 though if this sounded alarm bells that The Banshees were heading towards album band territory, they were unfounded. But there was a tendency for some clumsy lyrics (an otherwise excellent 'Circle', driven by some mighty fine cross-rhythms as Budgie battled it out with a tape loop, started badly with 'Pretty girl of 16 – has fun and runs crazy, ruined girl of 16 – now a mother grows lazy',) and the occasional filler like the fanciful 'Cocoon' (a Sioux choice stuffed with the sort of sexual imagery that frequently finds its way into her lyrics) and the cluttered 'She's A Carnival'.

By far the most intriguing track was 'Obsession'. Musically, it was their most successful departure from a rock sound since 'Voices' on the flip of 'Hong Kong Garden'. The claustrophobia created by the sucking sound on a backwards-running tape was a perfect accompaniment to Sioux's intimate whispers. The song did its subject matter proud: "It's a story a friend of mine told me in New York about this friend of his who just went totally off her head about this bloke who lived upstairs. She imagined they had a pact between each other . . . She'd actually sit outside his door and listen to him walking about and then break into his room and touch his things and leave a pubic hair behind." (Sioux)

No doubt had she met Nagisa Oshima in Japan, earlier that year, he would have made a film out of it.

But every dreamhouse has its heartache, and during the album sessions, relations between McGeoch and the rest of the group began to sour. He was not the tower of strength who had helped the group restate their credo so forcefully on 'Juju', although his reduced involvement as a composer didn't stop him delivering some imaginative musical contributions. After a couple of club dates in Madrid at the end of October, John collapsed and was taken to hospital suffering from nervous exhaustion. On their return to Britain, and with a full UK tour imminent, he went home for a week's rest. One morning, a letter arrived. 'Dear John . . . '

As McGeoch later put it, he'd been "dissolved out of the partnership." Steve told the music press, "The nature of his illness has been such that he can no longer make the contribution expected of each member of the group." It was vague, but after the all-too visible split in 1979, the group weren't prepared to wash their dirty linen in public a second time.

Though ego battles, particularly with Sioux, had been going on for several months, John's depression and a disastrous second show in Madrid – for which he carried the can – provided the group with a more tangible justification for the sacking. While McGeoch was left with a bitter taste in his mouth, Robert Smith found himself with a dozen new songs to learn in a matter of days.

The sacked guitarist eventually settled with Public Image Ltd, finding John Lydon far easier to work with than his former colleagues. Of his old boss he later commented: "She likes to surround herself with sycophants." It wasn't the first time such a thing had been said about a rock star.

From dreamhous

Robert Smith was an obvious replacement. Since The Cure supported The Banshees on the fateful Join Hands Tour, they'd built up a considerable following, enjoyed five minor hits and had a top 10 album in 1982's 'Pornography'. But Smith never quite severed his ties with The Banshees. In April 1982, news filtered out that he'd written a song with Steve Severin, which they intended to release as a single. The pair hoped this would lead to an album which they would record with guest singers. But as for Smith's

o bleakhouse

co-option into The Banshees, it was strongly emphasised this was merely a temporary measure. A spokesman for The Cure said: "Robert Smith won't be joining Siouxsie full-time. He and Lawrence Tolhurst will continue to work together and there is a four-track EP coming out in February, when they will do some live shows with selected musicians."

Smith was not so sure. By December, he was publicly posing the question many others had considered: Do The Cure really exist any more? Had he decided to throw in his lot with Siouxsie And The Banshees it is certain he would have been welcomed with open arms. But his chief concern was one of control. With all due respect to Lol, who'd been there since the 1977 Easy Cure, Robert Smith was The Cure. In Siouxsie And The Banshees, he'd have to take a back seat.

But for the time being Smith had little time to think about his position. Within days of McGeoch's dismissal, he appeared with the band on BBC's *Old Grey Whistle Test* performing 'Melt!' and 'Painted Bird' from the new album, then set off with them on an 11-date UK tour. For the first time, the group were augmented with additional musicians in a live setting, namely the Venomettes (aka Humouresque), the three-piece string section that had worked with Marc Almond on his 'Torment And Toreros' album. They played on 'Fireworks', 'Slowdive' and 'Overground', which had been dropped from the set since McKay and Morris' departure. Those who lived too far from the tour's seven stopping-off points could have seen the old favourite revamped on BBC-TV's *The Oxford Road Show*. Any notion that a string trio would bring stuffiness to the band's image was quickly swallowed: the all-woman trio came close to stealing the limelight from Sioux.

A signing session before the second Hammersmith Odeon show at the end of the tour was far more successful than the Aberdeen debacle. To this day, the group still make a point of turning up at one of London's major record stores when in town for a concert, especially as this usually coincides with the release of a new album.

The ups and downs of the past few years were beginning to read like a soap opera, something of which The Banshees were all too conscious. They were tiring of the same old British venues and an attempt to try somewhere new backfired when a second night at the untried Futurist Theatre in Scarborough had to be cancelled due to lack of ticket sales. Sioux thought the audiences jaded: "You get the impression that a lot of people are only there for nostalgia or because there wasn't anything good on telly that night." Perhaps it was the dry ice; or could it possibly have been that Siouxsie And The Banshees weren't quite the vital force in rock they once were?

"All these things are like little mistresses on the side. The Banshees are still married." (Sioux)

For the first few weeks of 1983, Siouxsie And The Banshees were put on ice. It was a good time for a break, allowing Smith to gather his thoughts, and Sioux and Budgie the opportunity to reactivate The Creatures.

Time
To Play

The pair opted for a working holiday and began scouring for recording studios in exotic locations like Bali, Columbia, Mexico and Central Africa. Finding these fully booked, or else far too expensive, they opted for the less commercial western side of Hawaii and booked a couple of weeks in the Sea West Studios, Oahu, previously frequented by the likes of Crosby, Stills and Nash and Marvin Gaye. Apart from the usual tourist requisites, the pair took off with only producer Mike Hedges as a reminder of life back home. Though a much needed holiday was the overriding rationale behind the trip, Hawaii also provided a refuge from the claustrophobic rock world. Compass Point this was not.

The journey got off to a fine start with no less than three New Year's Eve celebrations on the flight over. When they arrived at the studio, they found it suitably spartan and lacking any proper soundproofing; the only instruments they could see were drums and a marimba. A further search turned up a waterphone, a huge, wide-bottomed copper bottle with a narrow neck which was filled with water. Round the various circumferences were different lengths of copper welded on to the body, and these were played with a violin bow. It was just as well The Creatures had no great pretensions to be more than a percussion/vocal duo.

'Feast' was written, recorded and mixed in just under two weeks, which must have been refreshing after the traumas involved in the making of a Banshees' album. Whether it provided much more than a mildly lucrative holiday memento, though, is doubtful. While nothing so obvious as a Hawaiian guitar was used, The Creatures made much of the island's charms. The Lamalani Hula Academy Hawaiian Chanters sang on 'Morning Dawning', 'Inoa 'Ole' and 'Festival Of Colours'; 'Gecko' was named after an island lizard; and several songs featured many lyrical signposts.

The single that preceded 'Feast' was 'Miss The Girl', though the inspiration for this was apparently J.G. Ballard's novel *Crash*, rather than the island where the main rock idol was still Elvis Presley. The promo video emphasised the strong sexual sado-masochistic element in the lyric and promptly received an unofficial ban from the BBC – or at least, the producers of *Switch* declined to broadcast it. "It's just the two of us in a thing that we built which is mostly metal with nails sticking out of it, with dangerous elements in it, and the play off of flesh against elements of spikes and metal," complained Budgie. The sparse sound of 'Miss The Girl' went against the current trend: "I'm sick of all this wall of production coming out at you; it's really boring and predictable," lambasted the singer. Nevertheless, it proved one of the year's surprise hits; its number 21 chart placing was higher than any Banshee single since 'Happy House' back in 1980.

That same month, Sioux and Budgie returned to the studio to record a follow-up, a big production revamp of Mel Torme's 'Right Now'. In contrast to the starkness of the previous single (and its accompanying video), 'Right Now' boasted a lavish horn section and a fast, up-tempo dancefloor beat quite unlike anything The Banshees had ever done. Compared with this, all previous Creatures' recordings sounded like The Banshees without guitars. Sioux hadn't hit the charts like this since 'Hong Kong Garden', reaching number 14.

Nor had she appeared in so many teen magazines. None were particularly interested in The Banshees, though they lapped up the tale of Gregory Peccary. Budgie had heard about an adoption scheme at London's Regent's Park Zoo on a radio news story whereby a sponsor pays for the upkeep of an animal for a year. The scheme had been a success, but it seemed that no one wanted to adopt the pig-like peccary, so our benevolent Creatures dug deep into their pockets and came to the rescue. Animal-loving, film fanatic Siouxsie couldn't resist calling it Gregory, after fifties beefcake actor Gregory Peck. Later in the year, they adopted a second animal', Amy the armadillo.

Right on cue, just in case you thought those wild antics of yesteryear were gone forever, a news item appeared in between the lacy knickers and naughty vicars stories in *The Sun* newspaper. Apparently our heroes had arrived at London's Elysée restaurant at midnight with the likes of Marc Almond and some of his Mambas, Richard Jobson, and a couple of visiting Hawaiians to celebrate Sioux's 26th birthday. The ghost of the 1979 Rainbow concert must have come with them because by 4.30 in the morning, all hell had let loose with chairs and plates being smashed, and tables set on fire. But apart from bearing out the old adage that rock stars have far more money than sense, it wasn't much of a story. "It was all high spirited fun," said the owner. "The group come here often and they really enjoy the atmosphere. There was no serious damage done." The party ended up at the block of flats in West Kensington where both Sioux and Steve had separate apartments. Presumably no one dared set fire to the birthday girl's collection of masks!

Apart from a three-week tour of Japan and Australasia in February, the first half of 1983 was given over to the pursuit of extra-curricular projects. While The Creatures were spicing up the charts, the much-vaunted Severin/Smith collaboration was gathering momentum. However, The Glove – who took their name from the Blue Meanies' giant fist-cum-executioner in The Beatles' cartoon movie *Yellow Submarine* – failed to equal that success on two counts. Their timing was miscalculated, because by the time an album had been prepared for release, The Banshees had re-grouped for a short European tour ending up with three nights in Israel. On top of that, the product they ought to have been publicising wasn't up to much anyway.

The idea of recording a psychedelic pastiche was not new. Even The Damned's second album, 1977's 'Music For Pleasure', was touted as one. Psychedelia had been rehabilitated by the early eighties but – as in 1967 – all manner of rubbish was put out under its guise. Had The Glove stuck to their original plan of recording a single, 'Punish Me With Kisses', their solo indiscretion may have been excused. "We didn't want it to sound like a self-indulgent album made by two ageing hippies," offered Smith, already sounding a mite guilty. Later he came clean: "Yes, of course it was indulgent, which is why so few people have bought it."

When The Banshees returned to London from the Australasian tour, Robert Smith was approached by Royal Ballet choreographer Nicholas Dixon to score the music for a production of *Les Enfants Terrible*. Afraid he would be biting off more than he could chew, Smith instead suggested a smaller project where Dixon would choreograph 'Siamese Twins' from The Cure's 'Pornography' album. This received a public airing on BBC-TV's *Riverside* programme, where Robert and Lol were joined by Steve Severin on bass and Marc Almond's Venomettes on backing vocals.

Steve Severin

Robert and Steve returned to the programme in July to premier 'Punish Me With Kisses', which became The Glove's follow-up single to 'Like An Animal', issued in August. Neither song was helped by the vocals of ex-Zoo dancer and Darts' choreographer Jeanette Landray. Steve later regretted her involvement, while she recalled feeling very much a third party during the 10 days in June it took to record the album.

Its title, 'Blue Sunshine', came from a seventies' B-movie which took its name from a highly potent strain of LSD. But anyone expecting an acid-drenched performance must have been highly disappointed. Not even exotic instruments like the koto or a dulcimer could convince anyone this was going to be the Summer of Glove. In November, Robert Smith said: "There's been talk of us doing a 'Music For Dreams' album. A pure instrumental, but that's way in the future. It's just something we talk about in a drunken state." 'Blue Sunshine' wasn't a nightmare; it was like waking up and remembering nothing. 'Music For Dreams' never materialised.

When The Banshees reassembled, they had little to show from their lost weekend, bar one excellent Creatures single and a few reasonable album tracks. This was either a wasted opportunity, or else the sum of The Banshees was infinitely more than its individual parts.

Sideline projects usually relieve the inevitable sterility which sets in after several years functioning under one banner. Whatever the truth, the first Banshees' release since the spring hiatus gave them their biggest hit single to date. 'Dear Prudence', issued in September, confirmed the band as Beatles' interpreters par excellence and it gave them a top three chart placing. Like 'Helter Skelter', the song was taken from The Beatles' 'White Album', and was one of the few that remained relatively untainted by events in California in the summer of 1969. 'Dear Prudence' was a gentle Lennon song written in India and inspired by the sister of film actress Mia Farrow. Okay so Mia had the lead part in Polanski's *Rosemary's Baby* (shot, like Lennon, in the Dakota Buildings) but that was labouring it a bit!

Here's Another Clue For You All

Sioux saw nothing sinister about the alleged fixation: ''There is a special liking for that album. My older brother had the 'White Album' and played it constantly.'' Many complained that the charts were already congested with cover versions: ''To be quite honest,'' said Steve, ''there weren't any Banshees' songs written and we wanted a new single out. We also wanted Robert playing on it. It seemed a good way of getting back into The Banshees' swing.'' The finished single – which they had begun recording in Sweden in July, until promotional work for The Cure's 'The Walk' hit single took Smith away for a few weeks – was a stunning performance. It was as if Lennon/McCartney had written it for them. What they would have made of Budgie's first choice, 'Glass Onion', is anyone's guess.

The promotional video was shot in Venice by Tim Pope (who had previously worked with The Cure and The Creatures), but if the location didn't over-saturate the film, the superimposed water did. It was far more effective than the videos made for 'Spellbound' and 'Arabian Knights'. For once, the rich, summer majesty of the song wasn't ruined by tawdry images. The months spent pursuing individual ends had left The Banshees hungry to get back to work, but it hadn't entirely purged them of whimsical, half-baked musical desires. The B-side, 'There's A Planet In My Kitchen', was proof of that. It sounded like a leftover from the Glove sessions.

Despite the success of 'Dear Prudence', the uneasiness which had caused the group to branch out remained. The Cure were about to crest a wave of success in the wake of 'The Walk' and this thwarted any immediate plans to record a follow-up to 'Dreamhouse'. For the meantime, tours had to be carefully planned. The Cure headlined Elephant Fayre in August, then took off for a few US dates before recording a new single 'Love Cats' in Paris. This did better than ever, taking The Cure to number seven.

September was reserved for The Banshees and after returning from three dates in Israel preparations were made for two prestigious concerts at the Royal Albert Hall. Arrangements were made to film and record both nights for future album and video release. Within a month of the concerts, the double live LP set, 'Nocturne', had been released. The songs remained essentially the same but the band got extremely uptight when *NME*'s Mat Snow went on about Led Zeppelin, pomp rock and all that nonsense in his review. "Who doesn't enjoy a bit of good, old fashioned showbiz now and then?" he wrote. But The Banshees weren't in the mood for backhanded compliments: "It's really something we released as a snub to the bootlegs," said Sioux. But Steve rose to the bait: "It simply doesn't need defending," he argued. "Just because 'Nocturne' was a double live album, there's no stigma at all attached to that." And of course the all-important get-out: "We did it because we wanted to do it – the way we've always done things."

Quite frankly, they hadn't a leg to stand on. This was their 'David Live', or maybe even their 'Stage'. ('Pin-Ups' was to come later.) What everyone really wanted was for Siouxsie And The Banshees to stake out new frontiers, not dust off the furniture in an orgy of familiarity.

'Nocturne' was the group's first album on their own Wonderland label, which they had established as part of their renegotiated contract. After the split with Nils, certain legal matters had to be cleared up before the group could regain copyright of their songs, but by March Sioux was reportedly satisfied with their business concerns: "We now have the degree of control over our affairs that we always wanted," she swanked. But her stiletto retained some of its sharpness: "It's only come about by learning how this shitty business works." Our Outsiders on the inside continued to wave some kind of flag, even if it now seemed to be fuelled by playing devil's advocate rather than anything with real substance.

Wonderland gave Siouxsie And The Banshees that all-important identity within the Polygram corporation and was originally intended as an outlet for the band's talent-spotting. Thus far, the only other acts to appear on the label have been The Creatures and The Glove. Billy Houlston, who is now the group's PA, explained recently that this was because "they haven't discovered anyone they wanted to put on the label." The truth of the matter is more likely that the fanciful idea went the same way as almost every other artist's attempts to establish a roster of hand-picked protégés.

'Nocturne' opened, like the video, with an excerpt from Stravinsky's 1913 masterwork, 'The Rite Of Spring', a piece so shocking that it sparked a riot at its Paris première. Sioux did her rag doll dance, the live wires at the front pogoed en masse but fans the world over regarded the album as an expensive luxury. In the UK, it just scraped into the top 30, and remains the group's poorest seller.

The only winners were those who'd joined the Siouxsie And The Banshees fan club, 'The File'. Many members had been tempted by the promotional insert which came with 'A Kiss In The Dreamhouse' offering, for £3.50, a year's subscription and a package containing a specially designed membership card, badge and a newsletter packed with information, photographs and competitions. Also promised was the occasional surprise. In this respect, 'The File' came up with the goods at the end of 1983, when a seven-inch single was mailed out in a picture sleeve to all members. This coupling of live versions of 'Headcut' and a new song, 'Running Town', recorded on the second night at the Albert Hall, remains a unique item on the collector's market and the 2,500 fans who received a copy have recouped their £3.50 several times over. This 'Fan Club' single, as it's known, is currently worth between £35 and £40. And speaking of collectables, the souvenir poster/programme from the two Albert Hall gigs is a pretty hot item too.

Budgie demonstrates his Elvis Presley karate routine

"I'm as much of a member as I could be, but I don't have as much say as them. That's why it's always good when I go back to The Cure. I am The Cure." (Robert Smith)

Playground Twits

'Play At Home' was the title of a Channel Four TV series which invited several artists to record a 30-minute episode. Once mixing had been completed on 'Nocturne', the group extended their creative low with this mixed media offering of poetry, music, fairy and animal tales that climaxed in a burst of energy from one of the Albert Hall concerts. Each band member had three minutes to fill. Budgie recited an ode to Gregory Peccary; Steve reported on the role of an assassin; Sioux gathered some childhood memories, while Robert Smith imagined he was Franz Kafka. The sketches were linked by The Banshees and friends re-enacting the Mad Hatter's Tea-Party from Lewis Carroll's *Alice In Wonderland* (today, an acknowledged 'psychedelic' classic; the book even lent its name to a cult London club for mid-eighties' hyperdelics) but the overall effect was more a case of Alice In Blunderland.

On the musical side, The Creatures, The Glove and The Banshees all got a plug with 'Weathercade', 'A Blues In Drag' and 'Circle' respectively. Playtime ended with 'Eve White/Eve Black', 'Voodoo Dolly' and 'Helter Skelter'. Filmed at the Royal Albert Hall, the most memorable images are of a stick-wielding Sioux during 'Circle' and Budgie looking a dead ringer for T.Rex's Mickey Finn – but much cheekier of course. Among the bit-part players were Billy Houlston, Dave Woods, Annie Hogan and Mike Hedges though few would have recognised them under the thick paint and costumes.

By the end of the year work on a new studio album, which began during the summer, was nearing completion. Smith had recorded his guitar parts by November, and had put on his other hat to begin work on 'The Top', The Cure's follow-up to 'Pornography'. During this time, the remaining Banshees oversaw the transfer of the tapes to digital, added final overdubs and mixed the lot down at Roundhouse studios.

Having premièred three tracks from the forthcoming LP, 'Running Town', 'Bring Me The Head Of The Preacher Man', and 'Blow The House Down' on Channel Four's *The Tube* in February (a performance blighted by poor sound), they opted for the more studio oriented 'Swimming Horses' as the follow-up to 'Dear Prudence'. This piano/drum piece, topped by a fine vocal performance from Sioux, was a brave choice for a single and they couldn't have been too disappointed when it just scraped a top 30 placing.

The decision to release what many would regard as an album track as a single was a conscious decision, not only to go against the trend of guitar groups that were flavour of the month in the music press, but also to satisfy The Banshees' characteristic flouting of commercial convention. This has been a game they've played throughout their career; hiding from the categorisation of those who seek to pin them down. Most of their own idols perfected a balancing act which meant they could shift happily from single to album market, from commercial to cult, from po-faced to frivolous almost at will. Siouxsie And The Banshees sought to continue in that tradition.

Listening to 'Hyaena' then, and reappraising it now, the overall effect was hardly more inspiring than the previous year's individual projects. Ersatz Banshees were two-a-penny during this period, but why the group embraced self-parody with such relish was beyond comprehension. But they knew things weren't right: "I think about half of it's up to scratch. We were aiming for something that was almost impossible to try and get – an LP out of a band that didn't really exist. And Robert's desire to be a pop star ground everybody down to one of the lowest points the band's ever had. But I was really pleased with the way it came out. It could have been much worse." (Steve)

The complacency showed and the evidence indicated that minds were elsewhere. Sioux obviously wanted to get back to her new video recorder and catch up with the schlock recommended by her pals in The Glove; Smith was saving his best ideas for The Cure now that faith in his original band had been restored by commercial success; and neither Steve nor Budgie were fired with enough enthusiasm to assume strict quality control. The Banshees weren't improvisers and that the bulk of 'Hyaena' was composed in the studio speaks volumes. On 'Dreamhouse', the looseness of the sessions turned up trumps, but here indiscipline worked against them.

Robert Smith later apportioned some of the blame to the part of the process he was not involved in: "After The Glove and playing about with the psychedelic thing, it was time The Banshees got raw again and I thought that was the way it would go. It shouldn't have been 'A Kiss In The Dreamhouse Part Two'. Lots of stuff came from me and Sev just staying up all night, playing and recording this and that, really rough and very powerful. But then the production smoothed it all out."

A case in point was the opening cut, 'Dazzle', issued in June as a single. According to Smith, this began life sounding "like The Glitter Band or Sweet or something; really raw. And then they got in the orchestra." Rather than beat the guitar groups at their own game, The Banshees opted for the lavish string arrangement that obviously muted much of the song's power. Nevertheless, it still sparkled amidst material like 'Take Me Back', 'Pointing Bone', 'Belladonna' and 'We Hunger'. 'Hyaena' found The Banshees picking at the bones of their own carcass. It was time to find fresh meat.

While the group seemed bent on becoming mere shadows of their former selves, London's Virgin Megastore in Oxford Street had opened its own Chamber of Horrors with a series of wax dummies of some of rock's most visual characters. High above the racks of records was the familiar apparition of Siouxsie Sioux – all ghostly white, draped in studded leather, jewellery and her unmistakable plumage – taking her place alongside Elvis, Bolan, Hendrix, Jagger and the rest. One wouldn't have thought she'd have been particularly flattered, but Sioux actually helped out by consenting to have her eyes matched. Had the model been holding a copy of 'Hyaena', the travesty would have been complete.

Keeping the Bolan Spirit alive

The group played a few European dates in March, and when they returned, a UK tour for June was announced. In May, The Cure's long awaited 'The Top' album was released to critical acclaim, and the expanded five-piece line-up were busy touring Britain and the Continent. Sioux and Budgie decided to make the most of the spare time and jetted off to Bali. Luckily, Steve Severin was home to take an urgent message from Smith in Hamburg. The Cure mainman explained that his workload was becoming unmanageable and that while he might be able to help out on the impending tour, he'd have to be counted out for any future arrangements. The warning signals had been aired the previous October: "A lot of the time, I'm still trying to play John McGeoch's guitar parts and failing. If I went on like this for a few more months, I'd be the next one to have a breakdown. It's a balancing act, and as long as I don't fall over, I'll be alright."

What knocked Smith sideways was the continued success of The Cure. Trying to build on that while at the same time playing an active part in The Banshees proved too much. Despite the press release which stated blandly that the guitarist was suffering from "nervous strain and exhaustion," The Banshees weren't at all happy. This situation had occurred twice before and both times they were able to call on Smith to help them out. Now it was third time unlucky. He cancelled a couple of The Cure's European dates and returned home to rest. People began whispering of a Curse of the Banshee Guitarists. They still do.

Think that you k

w what to do?

Within a week of Smith's calamitous announcement, Siouxsie And The Banshees had located a suitable replacement in John 'Valentine' Carruthers, a 25-year-old guitarist who, until August 1983, had been a member of **Renewal** Sheffield's Clock DVA. The arrangement instantly worked well, according to Steve, but John's memories of his induction were obscured by the amount of work involved: "I had to learn about 30 songs in 10 days," he recalled. "It was horrible." At this stage The Banshees wouldn't be drawn into making any announcement regarding his status within the band. "We'll just have to think about it on the tour," said Steve. "Us and guitarists don't seem to get on very well."

The material was drawn from every stage of the band's career bar 'Join Hands' and Carruthers proved an adept replacement. After climaxing with a couple of nights at the Hammersmith Odeon, the next task was to prepare for the important American dates in July, their first since signing a new deal there with Geffen. The only real hitch occurred when Budgie was hospitalised after having a few too many vodkas.

John Carruthers' first test in the studio was to re-record Robert Smith's parts on a projected EP of cover versions which had been recorded back in July 1983 and was originally intended for release by the end of that year. Instead of raiding The Beatles' 'White Album' once more, they chose to restore some of their own work with the help of the Chandos Players string section. Among those contributing were Ginny Ball, Anne Stephenson (both of whom had guested on The Glove LP), Bill McGee and Martin McCarrick.

This surfaced as 'The Thorn' in October and pleasantly surprised even those who had come to bury the band. The incorporation of strings on 'Overground' and 'Voices', coupled with better production added power to both songs, though the re-recording of 'Placebo Effect' from 'Join Hands' was less successful. (And was that really 'Fuck you two! Cure my ailments' midway through the song!?) The final choice, 'Red Over White', came as no surprise. Though the strings took a back seat, this moody version outdid even the re-recording made for Richard Skinner's radio show.

1984 John Carruthers

Carruthers added some nice touches to the EP, particularly the double-tracked guitar passages which opened and closed 'Overground', but it was a shame he was low in the mix when 'Red Over White' exploded two-thirds of the way through. It could have been a disastrous exercise in nostalgia: instead it lay the foundation upon which a new, more confident Banshees would emerge. After a dozen or so European dates in November, the group used the winter months to reappraise their situation and begin writing material for the next LP. They weren't going to make the same mistake again.

1985 was the year musicians went charitable in a big way. Unlike many rock luminaries, who wear their habits on their arm like a badge, the subject of drugs never seemed to crop up with regard to Siouxsie And The Banshees; anyway, alcoholic beverages seemed to be their poison. But in April they played a fund-raising concert for Pete Townshend's Double O charity which had been set up to help heroin addicts. The group decided it was time they could be "counted among those who are concerned about the increasing use of heroin among young people." The cause was an appropriate one for a group that had spent nearly a decade struggling for the right of control over their music: heroin was usually about surrendering any sense of control.

Despite the fact that The Associates and Bronski Beat had already suffered poor sound at St. James' Church, Piccadilly, the band's passion for unusual venues outweighed those considerations and 500 people paid £10 per head for the pleasure of hearing the sound bounce around in all directions in what was The Banshees' first UK gig in 10 months. Siouxsie, the woman who had once said, "I just don't want to help people. I think everyone should help themselves," was later pictured handing over a cheque for £5,000 to The Who's guitarist-cum-philanthropist. Her previous simplistic attitude towards 'causes', which seemed to say that only animals and disabled people deserved special attention, had widened considerably.

The group broke rehearsals for their new material to play the concert, but by the end of the month were busy in Berlin's Hansa studios with producer Hugh Jones (who'd previously worked with Carruthers on Clock DVA's 1983 album 'Advantage'). Bowie's 'Low' and Iggy Pop's 'The Idiot' were both recorded there; a fact that was probably more than coincidental. The Banshees needed every bit of help they could muster, even if it meant Sioux and Steve getting sentimental about some of their favourite records.

Originally they'd planned to work with American Bob Ezrin but the relationship soured before they even entered a studio. The group were obviously determined to get it right no matter how long it took, so when a disagreement arose with Jones, he too was fired and the album was held up again. Officially the group's verdict was that he misunderstood what they wanted from the mixes. Other sources say Jones made the fatal mistake of playing the unfinished tapes to functionaries at Polydor which, in the eyes of a band who treasured their autonomy, constituted a flagrant breach of trust. Whichever way, he had to go.

The new recordings were put aside during the summer, and the group played nine dates in Italy, a country where they have a large following and always enjoy visiting. After two dates in August took them to Belgium and France on consecutive days, they began work on a new song, 'Cities In Dust', at London's Matrix studios with engineer Julian Standen. The lyrics were inspired by a visit to Pompeii during the July Italian visit, though uncannily, news of the Columbian volcano and earthquake broke during the song's period of gestation.

The original plan was to put the new song on the flip of 'Parties Fall', but as 'Cities In Dust' looked more and more like a single, this was scrapped. The video (once again directed by Tim Pope) that accompanied the eventual release of 'Cities' in October was the first to have been developed before they began shooting, and the usual problem of what role the boys should take was solved by making them pose as statues. Behind them ran striking footage of violent molten lava.

When another UK tour was announced in September, Sioux proudly stated it wasn't directly linked to a sales campaign. Not only did this bring undue

Sioux with Pete Townshend, handing over a cheque for 'Double O'

attention to the fact that all their other excursions had been, the release of 'Cities In Dust' coincided very nicely with the schedule as it turned out.

It wasn't massive, but the single did give The Banshees their biggest hit since 'Dear Prudence', and deservedly so. It was a poke in the eye for the knockers too as the band had managed to integrate sequencers, a drum machine and a fairly big production with their own sound and come up with something commercial, original and still sounding like Siouxsie And The Banshees. It was a pity they let Steve Churchyard loose with an 'Extended Eruption Mix' on the 12-inch. This featured an added percussion break and dubbed up vocals and managed to spoil the whole impact of the song. Unfortunately, 'An Execution', which conjured up the menace of 'Red Over White' but did nothing with it, and the instrumental 'Quarterdrawing Of The Dog' were both unmemorable flipsides. Nevertheless, 'Cities In Dust' meant fans could await the new album with some degree of optimism.

The group once again courted controversy when chain stores such as Boots, Smiths and Woolworth took offence at the 3,000-year-old picture on the label of the 12-inch which had been taken from a book called *Pornographic Pompeii* and captured a couple in a non-missionary sexual embrace. A compromise was later reached when a black sticker covered the offending point of contact.

A more serious setback for The Banshees came midway through the tour when Sioux collapsed on stage at the Hammersmith Odeon on October 24. Over the years, she had become noticeably more energetic in concert, but a particularly awkward fall onto a monitor wire during 'Christine' left her screaming in pain. Stage hands carried her off, though Steve threw off his bass, turned to the audience and shouted: "You've done this to her!" It was a strange reaction, but then his first thought was that she'd probably been felled by an object thrown from the crowd. A voice over the loudspeakers suggested Sioux may return if she was well enough, but before long, Budgie returned with the news that she'd been taken to hospital. Her left kneecap had to be snapped back into place, the leg was put in plaster and she was heavily sedated. Nevertheless, Sioux proved to be a staunch believer in the old adage that the show must go on and duly appeared the following night performing with the aid of a chair and a stick!

The group's next scheduled appearance was for BBC-2's *Whistle Test*. The seated Sioux, brandishing a stick topped with an ivory skull handle, managed to look witchier than ever as she turned in reasonable performances of 'Cities In Dust' and the as yet unreleased 'Land's End'.

Her insistence on continuing with the tour was to put back the healing process some two or three months. The imbalance caused by the plaster gave rise to a secondary complaint, a trapped nerve in her back, and Sioux had to continue with weights and physio treatment for several months in order to get back into shape. The tour ended with a special concert at the Royal Albert Hall on November 28, when old favourites like 'Hong Kong Garden', 'Mirage' and 'The Staircase (Mystery)' were revamped.

The most pressing business was to finish the album, so in December they joined Steve Churchyard in AIR studios to complete the mixing. If 'Hyaena' hadn't cooled some of the fans' enthusiasm, 'Tinderbox' would have been the group's most awaited album since 'The Scream'. It was certainly their strongest collection of songs since that time but only small pockets of critical acclaim were able to penetrate the preconceptions of most reviewers.

Temperature's Rising

The punk philosophy was . . . no Elvis, no Beatles and no Rolling Stones. Now the punk deities had themselves become clichéd and tiresome. Billy Idol had recycled trash into cash with the help of a James Dean rebel pose which won over the many thousands of American school kids who felt Rambo far too ugly a hero. The very mention of The Clash was enough to send blood rushing into the cheeks of anyone from the Blank Generation who still maintained a modicum of self-respect; while warhorses like Sioux and Rotten/Lydon were seen as just plain irrelevant. PiL plundered any musical territory they stumbled on with the sincerity of a confidence trickster. The Banshees, on the other hand, were far too stylised. Perpetually locked in their own wilderness, where dreams and nightmarish scenarios were acted out with almost calculated precision, they appeared to be trading on former glories in much the same way as Bolan had done during the mid-seventies.

Consequently, 'Tinderbox' was unfairly judged through a haze of cynicism which basically said, this is the seventh Siouxsie And The Banshees album: same as the other six. The grounds for this were obvious. In seven years, the group had not radically altered their style from the blueprint established on 'The Scream'. There were embellishments like orchestras, better musicianship, and the odd excursion into untypical territory, but still The Banshees sounded like they always had done. In that respect, 'Tinderbox' contained no surprises. But as an affirmation of the group's credo established almost a decade ago, it was a stunning performance.

A vital ingredient was the clarity and power of the production. The songs had been developed during months of rehearsals, so when they arrived in the studio, there was no pussyfooting around. Recording many of the basic tracks 'live' lent a much needed urgency to the material. No better could this be heard than on the opening cut, 'Candyman', which was issued as a single in February. Fuelled by Budgie's punishing on-beat, and featuring a fine interloping guitar pattern, this tale of child abuse/misplaced trust was probably the most confident display of archetypal Banshees since 'Playground Twist' back in 1979. But like its precursor, it proved too uncompromising to make any lasting chart impression, and stalled at number 34.

But those who couldn't resist the 12-inch, or who were quick enough to snap up the limited edition seven-inch doublepack, 'Candyman' brought with it two of the finest songs ever to grace their B-sides. Melancholic, yet magical, 'Lullaby' could have been an out-take from Jefferson Airplane's

'After Bathing At Baxters'. 'Umbrella' was in total contrast and was reminiscent of the soundtrack of Polanski's *Dance Of The Vampires*, with an Eastern-tinged heaviness topped by a fine wail of a vocal from Sioux. And to think those cuts were merely out-takes from the album! The Banshees were certainly hitting top gear again.

'Tinderbox' wore the classic photo of a tornado on its sleeve, and only 'Candyman', 'This Unrest' and 'Parties Fall' ("a brilliant performance, and a terrible mix – our lost cause, that song," said Steve) didn't allude to climatic conditions. Man's vulnerability in the face of the elements was a highly appropriate theme for a group whose past work drew considerably from the landscapes of human imperfection and the belief systems invoked as protection from the fear of the unknown.

The story behind 'Cannons', for example, was typical: "It was inspired by seeing a book programme about T.S. Eliot, I think. And it touched upon this freak weather period in the twenties, when it was either incredibly hot and oppressive or ridiculously cold. Apparently, in desperation about what to do, a cannon was shot into this oppressive sky every night in the hope of bursting a rain cloud. The image of this deserted town, with someone having to stay behind to fire the cannon, stuck with me." (Sioux)

While 'Cannons' appealed to their love of the bizarre, '92 Degrees' proved that their fascination for the murkier side of life had waned little since the days of pornographic T-shirts, Throbbing Gristle concerts at the ICA and of course 'Helter Skelter'. It was based around an unusual snippet of information; that, at 92 degrees Fahrenheit, more murders are committed than at any other temperature.

During the spring of 'Tinderbox', there had been much nostalgic media coverage of the tenth anniversary of punk. The artists still around from that time hated it, while many of the journalists asked to recall the era were obviously wracked with guilt. Guided by a light which shone 'No Future' into the faces of every music industry professional, wasn't punk meant to be a living experience, not something to treasure like a lock of hair?

Sioux sought to disassociate the group from the nostalgia and the post-mortems as much as possible but the knockers must have drawn some satisfaction from the band's performance on the 100th edition of *The Tube* in April, where they were introduced by seventies game show host Nicholas Parsons. No doubt the chairbound weeks spent resting the leg played its part, but watching Sioux conjured up images of Bolan circa 1975, Gary Glitter on one of his comeback shows or even Elvis's swansong on his last TV special. Her face had filled out and the make-up she had always employed to dazzling effect looked uncomplimentary. The songs, 'Candyman' and '92 Degrees' indicated a musical consolidation, rather than constipation, as the Quanticks of this world would have it, but the lasting memory is the burlesque image of Sioux.

It was a different story a couple of months earlier when the group accepted their first major film appearance, albeit in a cameo role. They had flown to Los Angeles on January 23 and a day later were on the Columbia film set preparing for a shoot. The film was Richard Todd's *Out Of Bounds*, but the part was hardly demanding. They were required to mime to 'Cities In Dust' in a Hollywood bar! It wasn't the first film work they'd been offered by any means, but as almost all previous offers were for horror yarns like *The Howling II*, and they needed the US exposure anyway, they accepted it. Apart from *Out Of Bounds* and *The Punk Rock Movie*, they have appeared in just one other film, *Court Of Miracles*.

After some selected European dates at the end of April, the band flew out for an extensive eight-week tour of America and Canada to promote both film and album. Despite employing the usual promotional devices, including a 'Tinderbox' interview album pressed by Geffen and distributed among radio stations, neither single nor album made a really significant breakthrough.

In their tenth anniversary year, Siouxsie And The Banshees made just one UK appearance, at the annual WOMAD festival at Clevedon, near Bristol, on July 19. Headlining on the Saturday night, they came on at around 11pm and played a polished set that included one new number, 'Song From The Edge Of The World', plus a rare live airing of 'Lullaby'.

Though the band had no desire to celebrate their first decade in the music business, hundreds of their most devout fans turned out at an unofficial anniversary bash held at the Electric Ballroom, Camden, almost 10 years to the day of the début 100 Club performance. Fred Robbins, who once used his redundancy pay-off to finance a "chance of a lifetime" trek following the band on the ill-fated Scandinavian tour, teamed up with a couple of friends and managed to persuade some 450 die-hards from as far away as Scotland, Sweden, France, Belgium and Italy to join in the celebrations. While the video films were well-received, a Siouxsie look-a-like contest was greeted with a resounding thumbs-down. Banshees' fans are obviously a far shyer breed than their Elvis counterparts!

Billy Houlston arrived to wish the organisers luck, then returned to the John Henry studios where the band were rehearsing to give a first-hand report. One by one Budgie, John and then Steve Severin arrived and spent several hours chatting, signing autographs and sampling the beverages on offer. Sioux missed out on this opportunity to meet the fans, ostensibly because she was busy in the studio, but Budgie admitted there were worries regarding her safety. Steve enjoyed himself so much he ended up staying the whole course, but ex-Sioux champion Jane Solanas (alias Suck) was less than enamoured. Miffed when no one recognised her, she proceeded to get drunk, then turned on the venom in a scathing review for the *NME* the following week.

She's Too Much For My Mirror

By the time the group returned from fulfilling a long-held ambition to visit South America where they spent two weeks playing to Brazilian and Argentine audiences (and watched sales of 'Once Upon A Time' treble in the process!), rumours had spread concerning their next 'secret' album, which had been recorded at Abbey Road's famous Studio Two between July and September.

The mystery began to unfold as The Banshees began the New Year in a blaze of publicity which entailed appearances on the children's show Razzmatazz, their first Top of the Pops since June 1984, Dutch, German and Sky Channel cable TV, an interview for the Mike Read radio show and a session for Janice Long. They also spent a couple of days in Portmeirion, Clough Williams-Ellis's dream village in North West Wales which provided the nightmare setting for the sixties' cult TV series The Prisoner, recording a sequence for The Tube.

The new single was a version of the Dylan/Band composition, 'This Wheel's On Fire', which had been a number five hit for Julie Driscoll, Brian Auger And The Trinity in 1968. Reaching number 14, it gave the group their biggest hit since 'Dear Prudence', ironically another non-original. But it was the session recorded for Janice Long which gave the game away. Alongside a great new original, a ballad called 'Something Blue', the session included a version of Television's 'Little Johnny Jewel'. Had These Foolish Things really recorded an album of cover versions? If so, they were setting themselves up for a roasting from the cynics. You could almost see them limbering up: having well and truly exhausted self-parody, they would write, Siouxsie And The Banshees had now jumped onto the revivalist bandwagon to save their flagging career. But before the army of savage pencils had time to sharpen up for the kill, the group issued their own disclaimer: "Part homage, part sacrilege," said Steve, just in case anyone took their bit of fun too seriously.

When 'Through The Looking Glass' appeared in March, few could disagree with him. But because most of the songs were dusted down remnants from Sioux and Steve's teenage fantasy years, they ended up with a set of faithful, if somewhat unmemorable recreations. One song, though, stuck in the mind as one of the most excruciating cover versions ever attempted. From the outset, Sioux singing Billie Holiday's 'Strange Fruit', a painful tale of black oppression, looked incredulous; but the addition of a Dixieland funeral march made previous descents into bathos seem respectable by comparison.

With the exception of a whimsical 'Trust In Me', filched from Walt Disney's The Jungle Book, the rest of the selections held no surprises. "A tribute to pre-punk art-pop," accurately gauged Simon Frith. Sparks, Roxy Music, John Cale, Kraftwerk, The Doors all received the Banshee treatment with varying degrees of success. Best were the lesser-known covers like Cale's

'Gun' (from 1974's 'Fear') and Kraftwerk's 'Hall Of Mirrors' (from 'Trans-Europe Express', 1977). Notable absentees were Marc Bolan and David Bowie. The former had already been eulogised with the version of '20th Century Boy' on the flip of 'The Staircase (Mystery)', but the opportunity to prove Julie Burchill right was waived. The project had already borrowed from the 'Pin-Ups' concept without pushing the ersatz Bowie accusation too far.

There was a simple explanation behind the recording of 'Through The Looking Glass': "As far back as 'Dear Prudence', we were considering putting an EP together of cover versions," said the singer. "The last two albums have been torture to finish, they've just taken too long, so we decided to have some fun and do it straight off." Had it been a cynical exercise to get hits which, after all, is the overriding rationale for most forays into rock's back catalogue, you can be sure they would have gone for more obvious material. In fact, the selection proved a difficult task, as Sioux explained: "The lyrics mattered. There were certain suggestions I would just not sing because the lyrics were dreadful." This excluded most of the Motown hits for a start. Among the other non-starters were Traffic's 'Paper Sun', Mick Ronson's 'Only After Dark' and Tom Jones's 'What's New Pussycat?' Roxy Music's 'Pyjamerama' and 'The Thrill Of It All' were both attempted before they opted for the less obvious 'Sea Breezes'.

The album looked all the more redundant when held up against Nick Cave's 'Kicking Against The Pricks' album released several weeks earlier. Not only did Cave choose his material carefully, he turned the songs inside out and reconstructed them tailor-made for his own needs. 'Through The Looking Glass' was what it implied, a voyeuristic exercise, with no pretensions to be anything else. The success of 'This Wheel's On Fire', and its follow-up 'The Passenger', ensured it a respectable chart placing but most fans treated it as a mildly pleasing distraction from the main body of the group's work.

Le

me out of here!

8

Despite decrying the attention given to an exhumation of punk in 1986, there was no doubting Siouxsie And The Banshees were busy conducting a post-mortem of their own. They had been trapped by their own myths, their image and, in many respects, their own musical style. While their contemporaries had long since jettisoned the baggage of a decade ago, The Banshees still seemed to be carrying the burden.

A major hurdle was accepting they were now part of the rock **Breaking** establishment. Siouxsie And The Banshees had what they wanted: a recording contract which gave them total musical freedom, a **Up Isn't** loyal following in Britain and on the Continent which guaranteed their continued existence and a highly professional back-up management unit which ensured their career ran as smoothly as **So Hard** possible. Rumours abounded that Sioux wouldn't talk to the music press unless she was guaranteed a front cover. Nor would she consent to a photo shoot unless the right to veto any unflattering **To Do** pictures was guaranteed. Complete control, or the wild excesses of a vainglorious prima donna? Their immediate task was to rejuvenate the band before they themselves began to lose interest; then to fix their sights on the lucrative American market which continued to elude them.

Even before the release of 'Looking Glass', the process of renewal was beginning. The video for 'The Passenger' featured a sartorially rejuvenated Sioux including a new geometric Vidal Sassoon hairdo. "Just a temporary image," prayed the *Dazzle* Siouxsie-zine. "She will be back to the gothic look by the summer."

But the split ends were just a start. A notable absentee from 'The Passenger' video was John Carruthers. Since January 26, just four days before Sioux's hairdresser received the call, he'd begun working his notice starting with an appearance on *Top Of The Pops*. Siouxsie marked the announcement, which came several weeks later, with one of her most pithy quotes: "We're like *The Picture Of Dorian Gray*. We continue unblemished, while the guitarists we discard bear all the scars."

Manager Dave Woods outlined the new mood of change in The Banshees' camp: "The others have decided they'd rather not tour, but want time to write new material. Their re-vamp will probably take about six months, which doesn't suit John. It will be a long time before the band re-emerge. What it will be like is something of a mystery to us all. I'm sure The Banshees don't know what direction it's going to take, but what will emerge on record, and in live performances, will not be singer, guitar, bass and drum orientated."

The immediate effect of this upheaval was the cancellation of a planned US tour. John Carruthers, who'd contributed much to the success of 'Tinderbox', planned to team up with ex-Gun Club vocalist Jeffrey Lee Pierce. Meanwhile, news of two other ex-Banshees appeared in the music press in the wake of the impending release of the band's pioneering session recorded back in 1977 for John Peel's radio show.

The Strange Fruit label – set up with the blessing of the BBC – had hoped to issue the EP before the end of 1986, but the continuing legal wrangle between the band and John and Kenny caused its delay. A spokesman for the pair said: "John and Kenny are proud of their recordings and are most anxious that they should be released." The problem, of course, revolved around money. When The Banshees joined Polydor, all royalties were put into a band account and this continued after the 1979 split until John and Kenny agreed to negotiate the compensation claim filed by the remaining Banshees. Three years after the split, they received recording royalties but the publishing royalties continued to reside in the Siouxsie And The Banshees' coffers as 'damages'. A compromise was sorted out and the EP was released in February.

It came at a good time for the two ex-members. One month later, Kenny Morris had a 12-inch EP called 'La Main Morte', his first recording since leaving the group, issued by Temple Records. John McKay, together with his long-standing girlfriend Linda Clark, had formed Zor Gabor whose début seven-inch, 'Tightrope', was issued in February. Kenny returned to the headlines in May when ex-Culture Club drummer Jon Moss caused a fracas at his wedding reception, held at London's Limelight club.

Most surprising was that it had taken over seven years for news of the defectors to emerge. At the time of the walk-out, many felt Morris and McKay had as much a future ahead of them as Sioux and Steve, if not more. After all, McKay had been the band's chief songwriter. But they were mistaken. The Banshees rebuilt not once, but on several occasions in the face of adversity. And they were about to begin the process again.

The rebuilding began in earnest in May when the group became a five-piece, having recruited multi-instrumentalist Martin McCarrick in April and Jon Klein a month later. Apart from being the third 'Mc' in The Banshees, the classically trained McCarrick had a good idea of what to expect – he'd worked with them as far back as 1984 on 'The Thorn' EP and more recently, contributed keyboards, cello and string arrangements to 'Through The Looking Glass'. His only problem was severing his association with Marc Almond, for whom he'd played since 1982.

There was no difficulty coaxing Klein. The lanky guitarist had come via Specimen, one of the plethora of Batcave goth bands who laid claim to a piece of The Banshees' ice zone. He must have been pleased with himself.

Rehearsals centred around 'Song From The Edge Of The World' which had been in the set for almost a year but (apart from its appearance on the recent Janice Long radio session) remained unrecorded. But not for long. In July, this became the first vinyl offering from the new-look outfit, and was featured on ITV's *The Roxy* a week later. Surprisingly, this single has the distinction of achieving the lowest chart placing in the band's history, two places lower than 'Melt' which, at number 49, at least had the excuse of already being out on LP.

It was the bad taste left by 'Through The Looking Glass' which lay behind its lack of success. The sound was unmistakable, though the return of Mike Thorn as producer tempered the song's obvious strengths with an exotic touch. Even the 12-inch 'Columbus Mix' made better use of the extra time than in the past. The two songs on the flip were typically frustrating. 'The Whole Price Of Blood' consciously avoided the more characteristic sound, but the cultural mish-mash with its sitar sounds and colourful percussion hung unsatisfactorily between being a song or a piece of mood music. 'Mechanical Eyes', with its heavy beat and cross-purposes vocal, was similarly uncomfortable.

The relative failure of 'Song From The Edge Of The World' confirmed that the music needed a radical shake-up though it was a year before they resurfaced with some strange fruit of their own. Before they could settle down to the nitty-gritty of developing a new sound, there was the usual round of summer festival commitments. The début live appearance of the quintet was scheduled for the Plymouth Rock Festival on July 18, on a bill that also included PiL, Spear Of Destiny and New Order. Contractual problems between the various groups' managements and the promoters developed, a new promoter stepped in, altered the bill and PiL and The Banshees pulled out.

Of the three remaining outdoor venues, two were in Germany and one in London. The German dates looked equally doomed at one stage when Budgie developed chicken-pox, but he recovered in time for Jon and Martin to début at the Waldbuhne Festival in Berlin. The following day, they played at the Loreley Festival, a picturesque venue high up a mountain overlooking the Rhine. Among the support acts was their old hero Iggy Pop on about his fiftieth comeback.

Lulu In

London

After several years of thwarted plans, 1987 saw The Banshees finally secure clearance for an outdoor London venue. Actually, it wasn't strictly a bona fide open-air concert, as it was held in a large tent set up in the middle of Finsbury Park. The bill, one of the strongest ever put together in the capital, contained some of the best and most enduring acts to have emerged since the late seventies. Supporting the group 'under canvas' were The Fall, Wire and Psychic TV. The latter were led by arch-provocateur and ex-Throbbing Gristle Genesis P. Orridge, who provided a few laughs when he walked on-stage dressed as Sioux.

This wit must have been infectious because days later The Banshees appeared on the children's TV show, *Get Fresh*, miming and obviously enjoying 'Song From The Edge Of The World' and 'This Town Ain't Big Enough For The Both Of Us'. Klein grinned like a Cheshire cat, the rest exchanged giggles and bemused expressions while Sioux toyed with her feather boa in the wind. Almost immediately they took off on a three-week series of US gigs which included a couple of dates as special guests on David Bowie's Glass Spider Tour.

Upon their return at the end of August, the group kept an incredibly low profile, venturing out only for an interview on the *01 For London* TV show in October. The importance of the new material was such that The Banshees took the unprecedented step of spending several weeks at Curtis Schwartz's residential rehearsal studios deep in the Sussex countryside. "It was so refreshing to be there," Steve reminisced on his return to the capital. Sioux echoed his sentiments: "It was a wonderful place and it's just a rambling old house with some giant-sized cats fed on rabbits. (We were there) just after that storm so it looked very strange, like an alien landscape almost, giant trees lying everywhere."

The first three months of 1988 were spent recording the new material at Marcus Music, London, and it took until June to finally come up with a satisfactory mix. A month later, a stunning new release was unleashed on to a world that was just beginning to learn to live without them.

The Banshees knew that all the latent experimentation with which they had been filling B-sides for several years with varying degrees of success would eventually yield something really worthwhile. 'Peek-A-Boo', issued in July 1988, began life as just another of these excursions away from more commercial territory, but with time on their hands, the group actually sat down and developed it rather than leave it begging for further improvement. The band, not surprisingly, blew their own trumpet louder than ever on the accompanying press release: "Let everyone else regress to the mid-seventies. Now, more than ever, is the time for an uncompromising Banshee single."

'Peek-A-Boo' landed right on the coveted spot where all great pop singles meet – that thin edge where invention collides with convention and imparts a whiff of fresh air to the stale odours that usually pass for chart hits. Mind you, it had taken them a year to get it right. While it relied heavily on studio techniques, the single wasn't simply a case of letting the machines take over: "A producer came in to remix 'Peek-A-Boo' assuming it was a collection of samples and sequences laid over a rigid drum track. But it's not at all. Most of it is played, even the stuff that is played backwards was recorded live forwards first. There are no metronomical sounds, it's simply the way we put it together that makes it sound so concise." (Budgie)

The underlying theme behind the song was not new, and if it alluded to the obscenity of advertising, it did so in a way that owed as much to Veronica Lake and Michael Powell's *Peeping Tom* as it did to Judith Williamson's *Decoding Advertisements* book.

"What 'Peek-A-Boo' is saying is that we're being presented more and more with soft-core porn masquerading as advertising and using women as accessories in a way that's nothing to do with images or with confronting people with their sexuality. It's designed to make them desire something that's unobtainable, and to change their values to make them dissatisfied with what they have, and want more. Sexual images of women in selling proliferate by the day and bombard the male population with an idea of a woman . . . (Steve) . . . that's available to them whenever and wherever they want them." (Sioux)

None of this was particularly apparent in the video which, like the record, was one of the group's best. Flickering from black-and-white into colour, the quick edits cut from Sioux, hair bobbed Louise Brooks style, blood red lips and in perpetual motion, to long shadows and masked figures providing the creep-show behind her.

'Song From The Edge of The World'

Mike Hedges produced both the single and the 'Peepshow' album that followed in September and the combination of the depth and richness which is characteristic of his work, plus the intricately structured songs penned by the group, resulted in the band's most lavish production yet. The riffing, the austerity and the claustrophobia that often permeated past recordings had been diluted; now the emphasis was on nuance and detail. Another important development was Sioux's voice, which responded well to the greater breadth of styles covered on the LP.

After the success of 'Peek-A-Boo', which deserved better than its number 16 chart placing, the group took the unprecedented step of releasing two further album tracks as singles. Both were wildly different again. Despite the absence of a T. Rex cover on the 'Looking Glass' album, Bolan's voice echoed in Sioux's larynx on 'The Killing Jar'. Though a more typically Banshee-style number with a marvellous chorus it was a shade too subtle to catch on in any big way.

The third single was like nothing the group had ever recorded before. A plaintive ballad, 'The Last Beat Of My Heart' enticed an unprecedented vocal from Sioux, and one that may open doors for further development. (The only performance remotely similar was on 'Something Blue' which appeared as a B-side 18 months earlier.) To call it The Banshees' answer to The Rolling Stones' 'Fool To Cry' would be an insult to Sioux's achievement, but as an indication of just how out of character it was, the comparison works.

The band took a considerable leap with 'Peepshow', a fact emphasised by the almost gratuitous inclusion of 'Rawhead And Bloodybones'. This boasted archetypal subject matter but stuck out like a sore thumb. However, Sioux's fascination with nursery rhymes was no less evident than before: the hoedown number, 'Burn-Up', faded out with an endless chorus of, 'Jack be nimble, Jack be quick, Jack jump over the candlestick,' while a line from 'Teddy Bears' Picnic' appears in the liner notes, probably as a reference to the winter fun and games in the Sussex woods.

The accompanying tour of the UK, their first in three years, matched the magnitude of the recent recordings and the faithful once again flocked in their thousands to the select venues which included two nights at the Royal Albert Hall. "I felt it was time to lose some money. We've been muddling along, not making or losing money, perhaps that was wrong. So this is a 'spend, spend, spend' tour. Go bankrupt for fuck's sake!"

In keeping with the 'Peepshow' concept, the stage set consisted of a series of screens which fell away at various intervals revealing a slightly altered perspective of the group. A ramp was erected behind the band which Sioux, dressed in knee-length boots, suspenders, satin hot pants and top hat, would wind her way up and down paying scant regard to the danger of further injuries. Whatever the cost, things never go exactly to plan. At St. Austell, the backing tape broke during 'Spellbound', forcing Budgie to keep the crowd amused with a five-minute drum solo; and on the first night at the Albert Hall, Jon Klein was felled by one of the descending curtains! Occasional mishaps continued to follow The Banshees during the European dates which took them into October. While in Ibiza, filming a rival to the vastly overrated spectacle of Montreux, a moth flew into Budgie's ear and had to be syringed out.

After a sell-out November tour of the US, where both 'Peek-A-Boo' and 'Peepshow' made a showing in the top 100 single and album charts, it looks as if the group are finally making an impression in a country which has consistently been reluctant to adopt some of Britain's finest groups. It took The Stones much longer than The Beatles to break, and apart from one massive hit, Marc Bolan remained a cult figure. Can we see Siouxsie And The Banshees joining the massed ranks of pop exiles? One would hope not, but the renewal process of the past couple of years has obviously

diversified their sound and has found them a new generation of listeners.

Siouxsie And The Banshees are far more at home with their role as pop stars today. The malevolent Sioux running verbal rings around Kid Jensen and Peter Powell is now equally capable of playing the genial TV show guest offering encouragement to groups as she reviews their promotional videos. But unlike their precursors, Bowie, Reed, Bolan and Iggy, you'll not find them singing a song extolling the virtues of rock 'n' roll. For Siouxsie And The Banshees, that would be going too far.

Appendices

Singles

78

AUG **Hong Kong Garden/Voices**
Polydor 2059 052; 1st 10,000 in
gatefold sleeve; number 18

79

MAR **The Staircase (Mystery)/20th
Century Boy**
Polydor POSP 9; number 24

JUN **Playground Twist/Pull To Bits**
Polydor POSP 59; number 28

SEP **Mittageisen (Metal Postcard)/Love In
A Void** Polydor 2059 151; number 47

80

FEB **Happy House/Drop Dead –
Celebration**
Polydor POSP 117; number 17

MAY **Christine/Eve White, Eve Black**
Polydor 2059 249; number 24

NOV **Israel/Red Over White**
Polydor POSP 205; number 41
**Israel (Extended)/Red Over White
(Extended)**
Polydor POSPX 205; 12-inch

81

MAY **Spellbound/Follow The Sun**
Polydor POSP 273; number 22
**Spellbound/Follow The Sun/
Slap Dash Snap**
Polydor POSP 273; 12-inch

JUL **Arabian Knights/Supernatural Thing**
Polydor POSP 309; number 32
**Arabian Knights/Supernatural Thing/
Congo Conga**
Polydor POSPX 309, 12-inch

82

MAY **Fireworks/Coal Mind**
Polydor POSP 450; limited number
with gatefold sleeve (POSPG 450);
number 2
Fireworks/Coal Mind/We Fall
Polydor POSPX 450; 12-inch

OCT **Slowdive/Cannibal Roses**
Polydor POSP 510; number 41
**Slowdive/Cannibal Roses/
Obsession II**
Polydor POSPX 510; 12-inch

DEC **Melt!/Il Est Ne Le Divin Enfant**
Polydor POSP 539; number 49
**Melt!/Il Est Ne Le Divin Enfant/
A Sleeping Rain**
Polydor POSPX 539; 12-inch

Discography

83

SEP **Dear Prudence/Tattoo**
Wonderland SHE 4; 1st 30,000 in
gatefold sleeve; number 3
**Dear Prudence/Tattoo/There's A
Planet In My Kitchen**
Wonderland SHEX 4; 12-inch

DEC **Head Cut/Running Town**
FILE 1; mail-order only to fan club
members

84

MAR **Swimming Horses/Let Go**
Wonderland SHE 6; number 28
**Swimming Horses/Let Go/
The Humming Wires**
Wonderland SHEX 6;
12-inch; limited edition poster

JUN **Dazzle/I Promise**
Wonderland SHE 7; number 33
**Dazzle (Glamour Mix)/I Promise/
Throw Them To The Lions**
Wonderland SHEX 7; 12-inch

85

OCT **Cities In Dust/An Execution**
Wonderland SHE 9; limited edition
poster sleeve; number 21
**Cities In Dust (Extended Eruption
Mix)/An Execution/Quarterdrawing
Of The Dog**
Wonderland SHEX 9; 12-inch

86

FEB **Candyman/Lullaby**
Wonderland SHE 10; number 34
Candyman/Lullaby/Umbrella
Wonderland SHED 10;
limited edition doublepack
Candyman/Lullaby/Umbrella
Wonderland SHEX 10; 12-inch

87

JAN **This Wheel's On Fire/Shooting Sun**
Wonderland SHE 11; number 14
**This Wheel's On Fire/Shooting Sun/
Sleepwalking (On The High Wire)/
She Cracked**
Wonderland SHEG 11;
limited edition doublepack
**This Wheel's On Fire (Incendiary Mix)/
Shooting Sun/Sleepwalking (On The
High Wire)**
Wonderland SHEX 11; 12-inch

MAR **The Passenger/She's Cuckoo**
Wonderland SHE 12; limited
number with poster sleeve
(SHEG 12); number 41
The Passenger (Lillllocomotion Mix)/
She's Cuckoo/Something Blue
Wonderland SHEX 12; 12-inch

JUL **Song From The Edge Of The World/**
The Whole Price Of Blood
Wonderland SHE 13; limited
number as a picture disc (SHEP 13);
number 59
Song From The Edge Of The World/
The Whole Price Of Blood/
Mechanical Eyes/Song From The
Edge Of The World (Columbus Mix)
Wonderland SHEC 13;
cassette single
Song From The Edge Of The World
(Columbus Mix)/The Whole Price Of
Blood/Mechanical Eyes
Wonderland SHEX 13; 12-inch
88
Peek-A-Boo/False Face
Wonderland SHE 14;
limited number with gatefold sleeve
(SHEG 14); number 16
Peek-A-Boo/False Face/Catwalk/
Peek-A-Boo (Big Spender Mix)
Wonderland SHECD 14; CD single
Peek-A-Boo/False Face/Catwalk/
Peek-A-Boo (Big Spender Mix)
Wonderland SHECS 14;
cassette single
Peek-A-Boo (Big Spender Mix)/False
Face/Catwalk Wonderland SHEX 14
Peek-A-Boo (Silver Dollar Mix)/
(version)
Wonderland SHEXR 14; 12-inch
Peek-A-Boo/(False Face/Catwalk/
Peek-A-Boo (Big Spender Mix,
audio only)
Polygram Music Video 080398 2;
CD video

SEP **The Killing Jar/Something Wicked**
Wonderland SHE 15;
limited number in clear vinyl, some
with gatefold sleeve (SHEG 15);
number 41
The Killing Jar/Something Wicked/
Are You Still Dying Darling?/The
Killing Jar (Lepidopteristic Mix)
Wonderland SHECD 15; CD single
The Killing Jar (Lepidopteristic Mix)/
Something Wicked/Are You Still
Dying Darling?
Wonderland SHEX 15; 12-inch

DEC **The Last Beat Of My Heart/El Dia De**
Los Muertos
Wonderland SHE 16;
limited number in gilded sleeve
(SHEG 16); number 44
The Last Beat Of My Heart/El Dia De
Los Muertos/Sunless/El Dia De Los
Muertos (Espiritu Mix)
Wonderland SHECD 16; CD single

The Last Beat Of My Heart/El Dia De
Los Muertos/Sunless
Wonderland SHEX 16; 12-inch;
limited number in gatefold sleeve
(SHEG 16)
There are also several interview
picture discs in existence.

EPs

84
OCT **The Thorn:** Overground/Voices/
Placebo Effect/Red Over White
Wonderland SHEEP 8; 12-inch;
number 47
87
FEB **Peel Session 5 DEC 77:** Love In
A Void/Mirage/Metal Postcard/
Suburban Relapse
Strange Fruit SFPS 012; 12-inch
JUN **Peel Session 5 DEC 77**
Strange Fruit SFPSC 012;
cassette single
88
MAR **Peel Session 5 DEC 77**
Strange Fruit SFPD 012; CD single
89
MAR **Peel Session 23 FEB 78** Hong Kong
Garden/Overground/Carcass/
Helter Skelter
Strange Fruit SFPS 066;
12-inch picture sleeve
MAR **Peel Session 23 FEB 78**
Strange Fruit SPPD 066; CD single

LPs

78
OCT **The Scream:** Pure/Jigsaw Feeling/
Overground/Carcass/Helter Skelter/
Mirage/ Metal Postcard/Nicotine
Stain/Suburban Relapse/Switch
Polydor POLD 5009;
inner sleeve; number 12
79
AUG **Join Hands:** Poppy Day/Regal Zone/
Placebo Effect/Icon/Premature
Burial/ Playground Twist/Mother –
Oh Mein Papa/ The Lord's Prayer
Polydor POLD 5024; gatefold sleeve;
inner sleeve; number 13
80
AUG **Kaleidoscope:** Happy House/
Tenant/Trophy/Hybrid/Clockface/
Lunar Camel/Christine/Desert
Kisses/Red Light/Paradise
Place/Skin
Polydor 2442 177; inner sleeve;
number 5
81
JUN **Juju:** Spellbound/Into The Light/
Arabian Knights/Halloween/
Monitor/Night Shift/Sin In My
Heart/Head Cut/Voodoo Dolly
Polydor POLS 1034; inner sleeve;
number 7

NOV **Once Upon A Time – The Singles:**
Hong Kong Garden/Mirage/
The Staircase (Mystery)/Playground
Twist/Love In A Void/Happy House/
Christine/Israel/Spellbound/
Arabian Knights
Polydor POLS 1056; limited number
with colour Sioux print; inner sleeve;
number 21
82
OCT **A Kiss In The Dreamhouse:**
Cascade/Green Fingers/Obsession/
She's A Carnival/Circle/Melt!/
Painted Bird/Cocoon/Slowdive
Polydor 5064; inner sleeve;
number 11
83
NOV **Nocturne:** Intro (The Rite Of Spring –
Stravinsky)/Israel/Dear Prudence/
Paradise Place/Melt!/Cascade/Pull To
Bits/Night Shift/Sin In My Heart/
Slowdive/Painted Bird/Happy
House/Switch/Spellbound/Helter
Skelter/Eve White, Eve Black/
Voodoo Dolly
Wonderland SHAH 1; double LP;
inner sleeves; number 29
84
JUN **Hyaena:** Dazzle/We Hunger/Take
Me Back/Belladonna/Swimming
Horses/Bring Me The Head Of The
Preacher Man/Running Town/
Pointing Bone/Blow The House
Down
Wonderland SHE HP 1; inner sleeve;
number 15
Hyaena: as above
Wonderland 821 510-2; compact disc
86
APR **Tinderbox:** Candyman/The Sweetest
Chill/This Unrest/Cities In Dust/
Cannons/Parties Fall/92 Degrees/
Land's End
Wonderland SHEHP 3; inner sleeve;
number 13
Tinderbox: as above, plus Cities In
Dust (Extended Eruption Mix)/
An Execution/ Quarterdrawing Of
The Dog/Lullaby/Umbrella
Wonderland 829 145-2; compact disc
87
MAR **Through The Looking Glass:**
This Town Ain't Big Enough For The
Both Of Us/Hall Of Mirrors/Trust In
Me/This Wheel's On Fire/Strange
Fruit/You're Lost Little Girl/
The Passenger/Gun/Sea Breezes/
Little Johnny Jewel
Wonderland SHELP 4; limited
number with cut-out sleeve;
inner sleeve; number 15
Through The Looking Glass: as above
Wonderland 831 474-2; compact disc

88

SEP **Peepshow:** Peek-A-Boo/The Killing
Jar/Scarecrow/Carousel/Burn-Up/
Ornaments Of Gold/Turn To Stone/
Rawhead And Bloodybones/The
Last Beat Of My Heart/Rhapsody
Wonderland SHELP 5; inner sleeve;
number 20

Peepshow: as above
Wonderland 837 240-2; compact disc

The Creatures

Singles 83

MAY **Miss The Girl/Hot Spring In The Snow**
Wonderland SHE 1; number 21

JUL **Right Now/Weathercade**
Wonderland SHE2; limited number
in gatefold sleeve; number 14

**Right Now/Weathercade/Festival Of
Colours**
Wonderland SHEX 2; 12-inch

EP 81

SEP **Wild Things:** Mad Eyed Screamer/
So Unreal/But Not Them/Wild
Thing/Thumb
Polydor POSPD 354; doublepack;
5000 in gatefold sleeve POSPG 354;
number 24

LP 83

MAY **Feast:** Morning Dawning/Inoa 'Ole/
Ice House/Dancing On Glass/Gecko/
Sky Train/Festival Of Colours/
Miss The Girl/A Strutting Rooster/
Flesh

The Glove

Singles 83

AUG **Like An Animal/Mouth To
Mouth**
Wonderland SHE 3; number 52

**Like An Animal (Extended Club Mix/
Like An Animal/Mouth To Mouth**
Wonderland SHEX 3; 12-inch

NOV **Punish Me With Kisses/The Tightrope**
Wonderland SHE 5

LP 83

AUG **Blue Sunshine:** Like An Animal/
Looking Glass Girl/Sex-Eye-Make-
Up/Mr. Alphabet Says/A Blues
In Drag/Punish Me With Kisses/
This Green City/Orgy/Perfect
Murder/Relax
Wonderland SHELP 2; number 35

Official Videos

Once Upon A Time: Hong Kong
Garden/The Staircase (Mystery)/
Playground Twist/Happy House/
Christine/Red Light/Israel/
Spellbound/Arabian Knights
Spectrum 791 506 2

Nocturne: Intro (The Rite Of Spring –
Stravinsky)/Israel/Cascade/Melt!/
Pull To Bits/Night Shift/Sin In My
Heart/Painted Bird/Switch/Eve
White, Eve Black/Voodoo Dolly/
Spellbound/Helter Skelter
Spectrum 040 191 2

Live UK TV Appearances

77

NOV **Make Up To Break Up** (So It Goes)

78

MAY **Hong Kong Garden** (Revolver)

NOV **Metal Postcard/Jigsaw Feeling**
(Old Grey Whistle Test)

79

DEC **Love In A Void/Regal Zone**
(Something Else)

80

OCT **Paradise Place/Eve White, Eve Black**
Futurama

NOV **Tenant/Israel** (Something Else)

81

MAR **Clockface/Israel/Spellbound/Arabian
Knights/Halloween/Christine/
Night Shift/Red Light/But Not Them/
Voodoo Dolly/Eve White, Eve Black**

OCT **Israel/Pull To Bits/Arabian Knights/
Sin In My Heart/Happy House/
So Unreal/Eve White, Eve Black/
Spellbound**
(live in Nottingham, 22 AUGUST)

82

NOV **Melt!/Painted Bird**
(Old Grey Whistle Test)

DEC **Melt!/Overground**
(Oxford Road Show)

84

FEB **Bring Me The Head Of The Preacher
Man/Running Town/Blow The
House Down** (The Tube)

SEP **Play At Home** (includes
Weathercade, A Blues In Drag and
Circle

85

OCT **Cities In Dust/Land's End**
(Whistle Test)

86

APR **Candyman/92 Degrees** (The Tube)

88

AUG **Killing Jar/Burn-Up** (Wired)

OCT **Killing Jar** DEF II, from KU-Club,
Ibiza '92

Radio 1 Sessions

77

NOV **Love In A Void/Mirage/Metal
Postcard/Suburban Relapse**
(John Peel)

78

FEB **Hong Kong Garden/Helter Skelter/
Overground/Carcass** (John Peel)

79

APR **Playground Twist/Regal Zone/
Placebo Effect/Poppy Day**
(John Peel)

80

AUG **Halloween/But Not Them/Voodoo
Dolly/Into The Light** (John Peel)

81

JUN **Arabian Knights/Head Cut/
Supernatural Thing/Red Over White**
(Richard Skinner)

82

MAY **Green Fingers/Cascade/Painted Bird/
Coal Mind** (David Jensen)

86

FEB **Candyman/Cannons/Land's End**
(John Peel)

87

FEB **Shooting Sun/Little Johnny Jewel/
Song From The Edge Of The World/
Something Blue** (Janice Long)